TRANSFORMED

TRANSFORMED

DR. KRISTI LEMLEY

BRIDGE
LOGOS

Newberry, FL 32669

Bridge-Logos
Newberry, FL 32669

Transformed
Live God's Best
by Dr. Kristi Lemley

Printed in the United States of America.

Library of Congress Catalog Card Number: 2021935873

International Standard Book Number: 978-1-61036-261-0

Cover/Interior design by Kent Jensen | knail.com

ENDORSEMENTS

Dr. Kristi Lemley possesses the personal and professional experiences needed to write on the rich theme of transformation. This great book is loaded with anecdotes, application, instruction, and encouragement. Every human being faces challenges and hurts, the residual effects of which require healing and forgiveness. In *Transformed*, Dr. Lemley shows the readers what they can do personally to move through these negative experiences, but she also vividly reveals God's part in providing life and a future. Expect to come away changed!

—**DR. CAROLYN TENNANT**, PROFESSOR EMERITA
AT NORTH CENTRAL UNIVERSITY (MINNEAPOLIS, MN) AND ADJUNCT
PROFESSOR IN THE DOCTORAL PROGRAM AT THE ASSEMBLIES OF GOD
THEOLOGICAL SEMINARY OF EVANGEL UNIVERSITY

Kristi Lemley draws on her own history of personal wounds, her graduate studies as a social worker, and her pastoral experience to provide a series of pastoral words of encouragement to the body of Christ. Each chapter invites readers to deal with issues that often lay hidden, deeply buried in their hearts. With professional insights, honed by years of pastoral care, she invites the reader to consider the power of the Gospel message to heal and transform their hearts as they continue to encounter Jesus on their path of spiritual growth.

—**DR. JOHAN MOSTERT**, PROFESSOR EMERITUS
OF COMMUNITY PSYCHOLOGY, ASSEMBLIES OF GOD
THEOLOGICAL SEMINARY OF EVANGEL UNIVERSITY

Do you need a transformation in your life? Then you certainly need to make *Transformed* your next read. Kristi Lemley shares real life examples from people who have been transformed by the power of God, including her own powerful story. She unpacks and expounds on deep Biblical truths that will help you not only overcome the hurts of this life, but truly live in the freedom and joy only Christ can bring. I highly recommend Kristi's latest book to encourage you and set you on your own path to transformation.

—**DONNA SPARKS**, ASSEMBLIES OF GOD EVANGELIST, AUTHOR,
AND FOUNDER OF STORY OF GRACE PRISON MINISTRY

DEDICATION

To the love of my life, Kraig, we have been amazed to see God move in our lives and I'm excited to see what He has in store for our future. To my family, thank you for walking with me on this journey. To my prayer team and board of the ministry, thank you for your continued support and prayers. Look what the Lord has done!

ACKNOWLEDGEMENTS

I would like to acknowledge my editor and friend Dr. Lois Olena. Thank you for making me sound better than I really am. To my mentors—Dr. Chuck Stecker and Dr. Carolyn Tennant your continued guidance has provided such wisdom throughout the years and molded me into the woman of God I am.

To Suzi and the whole BridgeLogos team, you are amazing to work with. Thank you for this opportunity to use my God-given voice to offer healing, hope, and victory to many.

CONTENTS

FOREWORD

Have you ever experienced setbacks, hurt, pain, disappointment? Maybe there are habitual patterns of unwanted behaviors or emotional cycles that seem to haunt you. Perhaps there are things lurking in the shadows of your past that occasionally show up in your present. If you hear the echoes of this in your own life, keep reading. We all have experienced the hurts and hang-ups of life and know others that have as well.

A transformational journey begins with awakening. *Transformed: Living in God's Best* brings the reader on a journey of personal experience with awareness-generating truths that bring exponential metamorphosis. There is an opportunity for everyone on the pages of this book to discover themselves and fall in love with the God who heals, the God who delivers, and the God who restores. There is a need for all to be transformed, and the journey of transformation is a rewarding discovery of the vast potential of what God can do in us as we still the roaring waters of life and sit down by the still waters of His Word and His presence.

As you embark on the journey of transformation with *Transformed: Living in God's Best* prepare to have God speak to you in the stillness of the words on these pages and allow Him to demonstrate His transformative power in your life. What weakness or insecurity might the power of God encounter in your life? What is possible when His power shows up? The transformative journey involves a surrender to His power and His work of freedom. Dead things live. Broken things are restored. What cannot be seen is now beheld.

The transformation journey with God leads us on a pathway of divine order—nothing missing, nothing broken, and everything in order. God's peace sets our lives, our families, our past, our present, and our future in divine order. No longer does one need to continue on in the torment of yesterday but you can walk in the liberty of an eternal, heavenly peace that comes from God's perfect, permanent work. Allow your life to set sail into the deep waters of His Word in the pages of this book and discover the possibilities that await you in your journey.

2 Corinthians 3:18 tell us that we are being transformed from one place of glory to the next as we behold Christ. What you behold is what you become. What you worship becomes who you are. If you woke up to find hopelessness and despair, consider what you are worshipping. Our perspectives and our worship are powerful forces that lead us onward. Through-out our transformative journey may we set our eyes on the victorious Savior, and the radiance of the Father. The Son of God has risen with healing in His beams. Turn to Him fully today. Let there be no shadow of turning in your coming to Him as there is no shadow of turning in His love for you. Turning fully to God means that seasons of refreshing are headed your way. He obliterates our past and refreshes us in His presence.

Be encouraged and set free today as you journey through these pages of transformation. May you find that your life is continually metamorphosized and the same grace you receive may be given freely to others around you.

—Dr. Zach Prosser, PCC
Lead Pastor, Celebration Church, Akron, Ohio
Director of Coaching & Program Development,
Emerge, Akron, OH
President, Zach Prosser Coaching

INTRODUCTION

Welcome to *Transformed*. This book is a culmination of my own journey, the stories of others, and my years of being a counselor and minister testifying to the transformative process of the Spirit. For years, I attempted to change myself and those around me while being a counselor. However, these attempts left me frustrated, discouraged, and at times hopeless because symptoms and struggles returned. Only through the Spirit of the living God at work in me did I begin to recognize that He alone could transform and heal completely. Psychology, the study of human behavior, provides some relief as it proves vital in my ministry to others, but it does not offer the full and complete healing that only God can regarding spiritual wounds. In conjunction of psychology and the Spirit, healing is possible. The brokenness that the enemy worked through to keep me bound was actually the avenue in which the resurrected Christ began to shine through my ministry.

Once freedom occurred, I thought that was it. The past would no longer entangle a person in their current context. Unfortunately, this was not the truth. Yes, the intense pain, negative mindset, and shame were gone, but a few issues remained. Residual effects from lack of security and godly love triggered insecurities and the limited ability to trust God. As a counselor, I began to once again recognize that this was not only the tape replaying in my life, but playing in the lives of those around me.

Why do we achieve freedom only to battle underlying core beliefs? Because inner healing is like an onion. As one aspect is released, there is another one even deeper awaiting the light of Christ's truth. Therefore, we continue to invite the Spirit to search within our hearts for any hidden, unresolved pain. This is the premise of the book. I begin by identifying that we all have experienced pain and trauma in which the enemy plants a lie that we begin to believe. In cooperation with the Lord, our wounds are exposed to truth, and freedom results. However, continued abiding in Him alone reveals who He is and what we believe about Him and ourselves. When our truth lines up with the truth of God's Word, then transformation results. This is not usually a one-time experience, but a process.

You may find this book similar to one I wrote in 2012 titled *Broken & Transformed: Moving Beyond Life's Difficult Times*, and you would be correct. After writing the book in 2012, many found the step-by-step process of healing beneficial. Time passed, and the book was no longer in print. However, I could not shake off the importance of it and the need to add more chapters and deeper insights. So, technically, this book is an expansion and regrouping of the previous version.

Are you ready to be transformed?

CHAPTER 1

THE NEED FOR TRANSFORMATION

We hide what we know or feel ourselves to be (which we assume to be unacceptable and unlovable) behind some kind of appearance which we hope will be more pleasing. We hide behind pretty faces which we put on for the benefit of our public. And in time we may even come to forget that we are hiding, and think that our assumed pretty face is what we really look like.[1]
— Simon Tugwell

One of the comments I heard over and over when people would walk by the book table and see my first book *Broken & Transformed* was, "I don't need that book, I'm not broken." At first, I was glad they had not experienced anything in their life that caused them great pain. However, over the years a realization began to evolve. Many people have no idea they are in bondage to their past, whether that be ten years ago or ten days ago. Sure, maybe they have not been sexually abused, addicted to drugs, or had a family member murdered; but they have experienced some type of rejection like being cut from a sports team, harsh words of a parent, betrayal from a spouse, embarrassment with friends, or abandonment. The bottom line is, we all are wounded in some way and in varying degrees. Something in our past or even current life has caused emotional turmoil, even if we do not recognize that it has impacted us at the core of our being, resulting in a change in how we view God, ourselves, and those around us.

Difficult situations we endure trigger questions which are a part of life. Why did God allow that to happen? Why didn't God provide? Why am I not a better man? I can think of multiple biblical examples that questioned life after experiencing pain such as David being chased by King Saul, the people in John 11 asking about Jesus not arriving in time to heal Lazarus, Peter questioning Jesus about John's future after being told he would be killed, and Job struggling with the day he was born. Again, questions are a normal part of life. However, it is how a person answers the questions that reveals whether they have allowed the wound to take root within their soul. This is only exacerbated when the person does not know the Lord when the incident occurred due to their young age or not being saved.

When a person turns away from the Lord's truth and leaning into Him, the enemy has the potential to plant a lie. The person begins to listen to the response that Satan offers, such as "You are the problem. You are not good enough. You are not a real man. You are not loved and never will be." If these lies coincide with what another human spoke or still speaks, then it only becomes stronger and truer within the heart of the receiver. This lie then grows into a core belief which we respond from. Our beliefs dictate how we interpret what we see and hear. This in turn causes us to react. For example, if you have been let down by someone, which left you feeling helpless, you may believe that no one can be trusted. This in turn makes it more difficult for you to trust God. If a father was gone a lot and never around, you may find it difficult to believe that God is always with you. If you were fired from your job, the lies that you would not amount to anything flood back into your mind and that belief is strengthened. These are just a few examples of a litany of possibilities.

An experience that occurred in my life as a teenager brought a stronghold of self-sufficiency that I was unaware of but with which I continued to have issues in terms of wanting to remain in control of my life. Instead of waiting on God to move, I would feel impatient and grasp the reigns back. This was part of the reason for my brokenness during a time of struggle regarding a church plant failure. When I became tired of dealing with this issue over and over, I asked the Lord to search my heart and reveal to me what was at the core. "Why do I do this? And Lord, please deliver me from it." This was what He revealed: I needed a ride to the high school to attend dance line practice. My mom could not get away from work, so she asked my cousin to take care of me. However, my cousin forgot. Cell phones were not in existence at that time, so I continued to wait. As time elapsed and the practice began, my anger intensified. Ultimately, I vowed to never rely on anyone else ever again. Yes, I know. A little over the top. But isn't that what happens when our emotions are intensified from anger, pain, or despair?

I thought all aspects of my parents' divorce were healed, including this incident. Sure, I remembered the missed practice, but would have never imagined a stronghold resulted from it. Yet, I was wrong. This was one side effect of the divorce that created a deep-seated lie and internal vow. Only during a time of sitting in the presence of the Lord was this bondage revealed. A residual effect transpired that also needed to be released. (I address this later in the book.)

Why do I share this story? If you have been able to 'handle' your fears or weaknesses on your own, you are likely unaware of the need for a heart transformation. I am not referring to the need for salvation but the need to be changed at the seat of your soul. God has a great plan for your life, and in order to continue to move forward, freedom in all areas needs to occur. Don't worry, the Lord will not bring more than you can handle at one time. The reality of inner healing may be foreign to you and even cause a defensive reaction. By the way, if you ever react defensively, there is a problem, but stay with me. Continue to read on.

Do you often find yourself having to address the same circumstance over and over? The people may be different, or the exact details altered, but similar emotions are triggered within you. I often say that the only way over the mountain or obstacle is to climb it and overcome it. We can attempt to locate shortcuts in order to avoid dealing with things, but it will continue to surface until we are freed from it. Why? Because that is how much God loves us. He wants us to be completely free! He wants to use your story to bring hope and healing to others, but this is not possible until you admit you are broken.

The point of this chapter is to help people recognize that there may be an emotional issue lurking deep within that needs healing. Yes, some emotions of fear are realistic, those we take to the Lord, and He strengthens us. But if there is consistent fear, insecurity, shame, or feelings of abandonment, then it is time to be honest with yourself. Instead of 'pushing' through another time of uncomfortableness or pain, how about allowing the Prince of Peace, Jesus, access to the depths of your being? He will shine the light of truth to allow you to see what lurks deep within your core beliefs.

It is okay to not be okay. Most people have been broken, and I would argue all of us will experience this at some time in our lives. Do not think that just because you have something that needs healing that you are in some way defective or insufficient in God's eyes. Brother or sister, it is just the opposite. God has been waiting for you to admit the need for transformation. He has longed for you to come to Him and give Him permission to heal. Yes, God needs our permission to allow the Spirit access into our pain. Only then can the power of God bring revelation, insight, and knowledge to areas that live in darkness.

The opposite of someone not knowing they need this book is one who knows they are broken and feel beyond repair. You may be asking yourself, "How did this happen?" There is a place where each person finds oneself at least once in life—a place of pain, sorrow, confusion, anger, helplessness, hopelessness, or any other describable negative emotion. Honestly, if you have been through it, *indescribable* is more like it. Being fully broken does not happen often in our lives, but when it does, it wrecks everything, and we are never the same. It is different for each person, as situations vary. One thing remains the same, though— the need for divine intervention.

Every aspect of our being needs transformation—our spirits, our souls, and our bodies. Spiritually speaking, we tend to run *towards* God or *away* from Him. There is usually no middle ground during this time. During my time of brokenness, I quit praying, fasting, and doing my daily devotions. This was my initial reaction. The questions I asked increased my anger towards God and the silence only created self-doubt. However, when things went from bad to worse, I knew God was my only answer. The choice to run back to God was the best choice I could have ever made. Did it make the situation go away? No. Did it make the pain stop? Not immediately, but it did change me.

When we run to the Lord in times of distress, then we *can* experience His peace, love, and faithfulness. I learned I was never alone. Even amid life-altering circumstances, my future was secure in my sovereign Creator. If you are hurting right now, run to God. He is there waiting for you with open arms. Nothing you do will make Him stop loving you (Rom 8:35–39). Some people may think, "But I created this mess." Yes, that may be true. However, you do not have to clean it up on your own. Allow the merciful lover of your soul, Jesus, to step in and take over.

Next, our souls—our mind, will, and emotions—need healing. Do you feel numb, in a daze, or on an emotional roller coaster? You might be confused as to how something happened, such as if your wife had an affair. You may hold yourself accountable if you caused a car accident, or you may blame someone else if they harmed your child. There might not be answers for your questions if a loved one contracted COVID-19 or was diagnosed with cancer. In most cases, a person's ability to function is limited in some way. Mentally, you may continue to replay the situation over and over in your thoughts. Emotionally, you may feel overwhelmed and unable to work. Your desire to accomplish other tasks diminishes, and all you can do is sit around.

As you invite the Spirit to help you, your state of disarray or confusion will level out. It might be extremely difficult to trust anyone or anything because you cannot change the situation or fix it. As you lean into the Lord, these emotions and thoughts will eventually decrease.

Is the will to live removed or limited? If this is the case, please reach out for help. Do not walk this road alone. As a matter of fact, do not think you have to figure everything out. The will to work or leave home may be impacted also. Again, reach out. Do not approach this daunting task alone. This is the reason the Lord has called us into community. Pick up the phone and call someone, perhaps a pastor or counselor.

Woundedness does not only impact our spiritual walk and mental or emotional health, but it takes a toll on us physically. Our physical bodies need a touch from the Lord also. I can remember being physically sick, vomiting because I was so stressed. Blood pressure may increase. If someone is diabetic, a trial could throw off their blood sugar. Some people turn to food in times of distress, so weight gain can occur or even the opposite where people quit eating and lose vast amounts of weight. Even David said his bones were wasting away under the pressure of guilt after being confronted by Nathan the prophet (Psalm 32:3–5). Turning to the Lord will bring peace to a weary soul and level out physical concerns prompted by stress.

If you currently feel overwhelmed and are struggling with someone or something, here is a list of suggestions to help immediately:

1. Spend twenty minutes a day by yourself praying, meditating on God's Word, just being still, or going to church. Even Jesus pulled away by Himself to pray and be alone with His Father.
2. Ask others to pray for you and with you. It is always encouraging to know that someone has you covered in prayer.

3. Only share with a few people you trust the depth of what you are experiencing. This will limit gossip or having to retell the story, which only engrains it further into your soul. By limiting whom you tell, you also can avoid confusion from differing opinions and advice.

4. Accept grace. The enemy wants you to beat yourself up and self-destruct. Do not try to get everything taken care of immediately. Oftentimes, as pressure builds, there is a reaction that nothing can wait. This is a lie. Things can wait—maybe not some things, but the majority can. Realize that you may not be able to do what you normally do at this time. That is okay. Do not add further commitments to your schedule.

5. Only focus on important things at this time. Keep God first, and give attention to other things like taking care of your children, working, or paying bills.

6. Make sure to utilize self-care such as getting enough sleep, eating healthy, and exercising. Physical activity can help decrease the pent-up stress your body may be experiencing.

7. Engage in life-giving activities. These will differ for people but can range from cleaning, hiking, fishing, reading, shopping, painting, or walking on the beach.

8. Keep a gratitude journal. Write down things for which you are thankful. In addition, add how you see God moving on your behalf outwardly or how you are changing inwardly during this time.

The bottom line is, we are all broken vessels—some more wounded than others. However, we all know the 'potter,' God, who will put us back together as we are the clay in His hands (Isaiah 64:8). Friend, there is hope. Yes, this too shall end if you 'remain on the potter's wheel' and do not remove yourself before you have gone through the process.

Do you know the actual process of pottery? First, the clay is shaped into the desired state. This can be very messy as the clay works through the hands of the potter. Then, the form must be fired. The pot must be heated to an extremely high temperature around 850 degrees Fahrenheit for about twelve hours. This removes water from the clay to harden it into shape. Next, the pot is painted with a glaze to add color and beauty by covering the drab clay. Once again, the pot must be heated to melt the glaze and create a seal. This time, though, the temperature is gradually raised in order to get it to at least 2,500 degrees Fahrenheit. It could not withstand the heat if it began that hot. Last, once the pot is done, the bottom must be filed so it can sit evenly on a surface. Wow, what a process.

How does that process relate to woundedness? First, we must allow the Lord to shape us based on how He has created us. Our callings, giftings, and personalities all come together to form a pot for just the right use, whether a pitcher, bowl, glass, or vase. It is during the fire of testing and trials where things that would cause us to be weak, unable to stay together, or withstand use (like the removal of water in the actual pottery process) are removed. Strongholds, bondages, and wrong mindsets must be demolished for the truth of the gospel to hold us together. Once our time of hardship ends, the Lord then paints us beautifully with glaze so His light can shine through us. Yet, once again, we must return to the kiln. This time, the heat is slowly turned up on us. He reveals situations that remain stumbling blocks, shatters any lies we continue to believe, and alters our core beliefs to reflect who God says He is and who we are in Him. Then, just as the pot returns to room temperature and goes through another filing on the bottom, so too our foundations must be firmly set on God's Word and on Jesus as our Savior. Once that happens, we are God's workmanship, ready for display and use. Then and only then will the God of the 'potter' get the glory for a product that is beautiful and useful.

What does the power of God look like in splintered lives? Keep reading, and you will see the reflection of His glory in the glaze on many lives.

CHAPTER 2

THE POWER OF GOD

"The same Jesus Who turned water into wine
can transform your home, your life, your family, and
your future. He is still in the miracle-working business,
and His business is the business of transformation."
—Adrian Rogers

The transformative power of the Lord is real. We see it over and over in biblical stories, but one example is Peter. He denied Jesus, yet when filled with the Spirit, Peter preached, and 3,000 souls were added to the kingdom of God on the Day of Pentecost and then another 5,000 just a short time thereafter. Mary of Magdalene, who had seven demons, was delivered and then served Jesus and was even present at His death and resurrection. The demon-possessed man in the region of the Gerasene's who lived in the tombs and called himself "Legion—for we are many" was delivered and then wanted to follow Jesus but was instructed to testify in his region to bring truth to the people.

These are not stories of physical healing, which are great, but testimonies that changed the way these individuals thought, felt, and believed. What happens when the power of God encounters our weakness, our past hurts, and the lies that we have believed? Freedom! A release from the pressure and lies that bind transpires. This chapter recounts a few experiences where the trajectory of lives were altered in one moment of time with a collision that turned into a life-long heart dedication and passion to serve the Lord.

I have witnessed this power and grace in my own life as well as in those of countless others. The Word of God says that we overcome by the blood of the Lamb and by the word of our testimony (Revelation 12:11). We cannot overcome without Jesus. Psychology even with all its benefits, itself will not fully transform us spiritually, mentally, or emotionally. I have seen some lives change in counseling through certain techniques or methods, but the change did not last. This is the struggle that psychology has when dealing with invisible wounds that we experience. Modern psychology is good at the research of human behaviors like trauma and development but lacks efficiency in addressing guilt, shame, and other spiritual wounds that must be addressed with spiritual insight. Counseling can be very effective in helping people with a variety of issues, but some wounds are beyond the healing reach of psychotherapy. It is not an either or picture, but a both and scenario because it is the truth of the Word that produces lasting conversion regarding wounds with a spiritual root. With this understanding, it is time to display how God worked in a few lives, including my own. More transformational stories will be shared throughout the book.

MY STORY

I grew up in a Christian home as the youngest of three girls. I can remember praying by my bedside at night with my mom and sisters or sitting on the register with a blanket over us as we read Bible stories. What seemed like an idyllic childhood hid the pain of sexual abuse. Then the storybook family disintegrated when my parents divorced. The family unit I knew was torn apart as my oldest sister moved out, my middle sister lived with my dad, and I moved away with my mom. I knew the Lord but turned to relationships with boys and alcohol to numb the pain, which brought on even more issues. I was able to forgive those who hurt me, but thoughts of *I should have known better* than to respond the way I did to the pain that gripped me brought about feelings of self-hatred. Anger, depression, feelings of abandonment, feeling unworthy of love, and a mindset of regret tormented my thoughts. Honestly, I would even pass out from drinking too much or from being high smoking marijuana while holding my Bible. Fear penetrated my being, but I knew that reading Scripture was my only answer.

Time passed, and I graduated with my master's degree in social work and opened my own counseling practice. The intense pain was gone, and I was happily married. One day after counseling a lady who had been sexually abused, I became angry. I did not understand why until the Lord revealed the stronghold of guilt and shame that I secretly carried. See, I was wearing a mask. I thought, if everything on the outside appeared normal, then somehow, I must be okay. I began to pray and ask the Lord to break the bondage. I wanted to be free. After praying for eight months, I experienced the Lord's miraculous deliverance. The dam broke, the weight of my shame lifted, and a joy that I had never felt before erupted in my spirit. First, I wept profusely. Then I began shouting "Praise the Lord!". That day I vowed to tell everyone about His saving grace. Long story short, a ministry was birthed that day, and pain turned into purpose. Only the Lord brought revelation, insight, and freedom. My life that was bound became free, and it was okay to be me.

I would love to say that was the only time in my life when God needed to transform me, but it was not. Another time, I was leading a church plant. I was an ordained minister and had been in ministry for over seven years. I knew I was not to pastor the new church but thought only to plant it. I spent almost a year in this city, prayer-walking the streets, meeting new people, leading a small Bible study, offering free counseling, and dining at local restaurants where I would pray with people. Unfortunately, the Lord instructed me to close the plant. A minister in a nearby city who was a friend visited me and gave me a prophetic word—that women who miscarry sometimes blame themselves, but they should not. This word did little to fend off the feelings of failure. I had to find other employment quickly and found a full-time job as a counselor again.

At the same time that the church plant was ending, my husband and I were attempting to sell our home and build another. The pressure of building a new home triggered my husband to become stressed, and he had to take an extended vacation, which brought on further negative feelings of helplessness because I could not alleviate his anxiety. There I was, left by myself to take care of two homes, work a new job, and cope with intense feelings of failure. Confusion as to why the Lord would send me to a city and then close the plant triggered isolation and abandonment. I was completely broken and overwhelmed. I thought that my dreams—the God-given dreams of ministry—were over, and I would live the rest of my days in mediocracy.

But once again, God came to my rescue. Day by day, He met me in my pain and breathed life and strength into me. There was one day, however, that changed the way I saw everything. What was the *truth* of the plant? I was only called to *plow the ground*. My prophetic voice was to speak life and push back the darkness that had encroached on this little town. I was never to launch the church, only speak *life*, day in and day out. This truth, while the church plant did not meet my expectations, transformed how I viewed the rest of my life. Sometimes, our expectations are what cause us to be broken. During this time, I chose to press into God. Eventually, the situation that broke me catapulted me into my destiny, and this book is a result—once again proving that God turns all things into the good for those who love Him and are called according to His purpose (Romans 8:28).

NANCY

The next story is of a dear friend, Nancy. She grew up in a typical family with loving parents and was a daddy's girl. She gave her heart to the Lord at a Jimmy Swaggart revival while in high school. She met a man in college whom she married. He became demanding and wanted to start a family immediately. However, feeling trapped, Nancy decided to divorce him. Freedom felt good at first, but it led to other poor choices and feelings of shame, fear, depression, and anger. The only thing she was sure of was that God had called her to teach, so she focused on her career. Feelings of loneliness drove her into the arms of another man who loved her. Unfortunately, unfilled dreams prompted another divorce.

Now she found herself divorced a second time and felt like a failure for not living up to God's standards.

Nancy was invited to sing in a choir, and she thought it would be a good activity to occupy some of her time. Little did she know that God was about to move in her life. One Sunday morning she ran down to the altar for healing from the pain of her past. At that moment she felt a release. God began a work in her, and over the next six years a deep relationship with Him resulted. Eventually, the Lord led Nancy to lead a divorce recovery support group. Her depth of freedom has brought hope and healing to many people who go through a divorce by her sharing her own story. One of her heart's desires is to tell others how God can and will meet their every need. Currently, she is the prayer coordinator for my ministry. Only God could take poor choices and turn them to bring hope and healing to others.

KRAIG

Kraig was a happily married man. His life was stable, and hanging out with friends was the norm until his wife drastically changed her life by quitting her job to go into full-time ministry, saying she was directed by the Lord. However, she made this decision without consulting him, which brought about anger and confusion. Stress from these changes triggered anxiety. Kraig began contemplating leaving his wife.

One day, Kraig went fishing with his friend, and it happened to be a very windy day. He quickly left the boat to go play golf. At 4:30 the next morning, he woke up and realized the boat was not tied up at the dock. He went to check, and it was gone. Thinking that maybe the boat had blown into one of the coves on either side of the home, he grabbed a flashlight and proceeded down to the lake. However, the boat was not at either location. He went back inside, knelt down, and cried out to the Lord. He told the Lord he needed help and guidance to deal with his stress. At this point, he was more concerned with his marriage than the boat. He then got up and went back outside.

The full moon shone over the lake. The shadows from the trees across the lake hid what lay beneath it. The water was still and the lake calm at this point as the wind had died down after sunset. Suddenly, something caught Kraig's eye—the boat! It began to cross the lake, on its own, right in front of him with everything still in it—motor, battery, life jackets, and poles. The boat traveled up to him and the dock. It actually even turned parallel to the dock, and all he had to do was grab the rope and tie it up. Instantly, he knew the Lord revealed His power and that his wife was following the plan of God. This brought great peace, and the stress melted off him. As soon as his wife woke up, he shared what God had done for him and how he knew she was being obedient to the Lord. He is now a staunch supporter of her. What the enemy attempted to use to destroy a marriage, the Lord brought revelation through a miraculous circumstance. God heard the cries of Kraig's heart and brought the answer he so desperately needed.

All these stories share the same conclusion—that God has the ability and desire to powerfully impact lives. What is impossible with men and women is possible with God. God is also no respecter of persons. What He has done for all of the above people, He can do for you.

Repeatedly, though, I hope you recognize that it was not just one moment when absolutely everything was different. Yes, the weight of the world was removed at times, and shame was erased.

Fears were alleviated, and love was experienced. However, there was a *continued process of healing.* I call it the onion effect. When one aspect is healed, chances are there is another layer that needs to be addressed.

God will not overwhelm us with everything at once. I believe that at times, healing of one emotion allows the Lord deeper access to another emotion. We learn to trust the Lord to go to the hidden, secret places when He has proven faithful previously.

In addition, we must do our part. We need to allow the work to be complete. Yes, we can stop the process at any time. Hunger for truth must dismantle the masks we wear. Relinquishment of fear, shame, guilt, anger, and unforgiveness is necessary and required. Just as Paul states in Romans 12:2 we must allow the Word of God to renew our thinking and expose lies so we may know what God's will is for our lives.

This book is a tool to help you invite the Spirit into your life and heart to transform every place of pain. Just like Nancy, Kraig, and me, you too can be completely freed and delivered to be released into your destiny and purpose. The choice is yours. Are you willing to invest time and energy to go deeper with the Lord? Or will you choose to stay right where you are, stuck? What will you choose?

If you chose to move forward, I applaud you. I know it is not easy. If it were, everyone would do it. You have chosen the correct journey. The path where life abounds and freedom is the result.

CHAPTER 3

PERFECT PEACE

"One of the rich fruits of anchoring ourselves in the inexhaustible love of God is that God heals our image of who he is."²
— Peter Scazzero

This comment is true in my life, and I feel confident it is also true in yours. When we center our minds on how loved we truly are by the Lord, then it dissipates our anger and increases our eagerness to reach out to Him because we trust His character.

JIM

Jim grew up in a small town and attended church. He was married, had two children, and a great job; however, he had walked away from his relationship with the Lord. His wife was involved in an accident, which created a point of crisis in their marriage. She informed Jim that she did not love him anymore and wanted a divorce. They immediately went to counseling for over a year until the counselor told them they were wasting their time and money because there had been no improvement.

Jim was about to lose his marriage and was desperate. The foreman on a construction site attempted to share Jesus with Jim, yet he continued to refuse. Jim stated that pride kept him from receiving the Lord at the time. He thought, "I can do it myself." After a couple of weeks, Jim cried out to God saying he wanted to die. He was hopeless, distraught, angry, depressed, and helpless. He no longer wanted to live. Within fifteen minutes, Jim drove to the construction site of the foreman, asked for help, and accepted Jesus. He stated that it felt like the weight of an entire building was removed and thrown off; he felt like he could have floated in the air. There was a release of pride, sin, shame, and guilt.

Briefly after Jim's salvation, he began to tell everyone what Jesus did for him. He became an evangelist on the job site, and his passion for the Lord grew. It was a process over several years of healing and transformation for Jim's relationship with the Lord to deepen. It was not until ten years later through God ordained circumstances, that Jim said another yes to the Lord and entered formal ministry. One of the best outcomes of this story is that Val, Jim's wife, accompanied him in taking ministerial courses, and they were ordained together. The lives the enemy meant to destroy have become a powerful team for the kingdom of heaven. Jim and his wife co-pastor a church and run a successful store that supports missionaries worldwide.

Jim's story and the stories in the previous chapter of how God healed and transformed people regarding their past reveal His ability is nothing but miraculous. How could these individuals let go of anger, depression, grief, resentment, betrayal, guilt, shame, fear, and a myriad of other negative emotions and situations?

They embraced the love of God by finding peace with Him. This realization did not come from a knowing in their mind but from a sense of the overwhelming presence of the Lord wanting to reveal who He is and His desire for intimate fellowship with them.

The depth of pain from the past can impact one's willingness to reach toward God. What complicates the issue even further is if unforgiveness remains. One can tend to lash out at the Lord for not having stopped a situation or preventing it altogether. Or, if we place the blame directly on ourselves for the crisis, then guilt and shame muddy the water further.

All these perspectives must be brought before the throne and processed. Yes, processed. This task is not completed with one step. I would even dare to say not even at one moment in time. Although spiritual strongholds can be broken in a second, deep-seated core beliefs must be challenged. Minds need renewal to grasp the truth of what is unveiled in the Word of God. You may have heard these truths before; however, it takes the power of the Holy Spirit to transfer them from our minds to our hearts—from the head knowledge of them to the experiential depths of our soul.

Calling out to the Lord for help remains a necessity. Are you angry at the Lord? Are you offended that He allowed something to happen to you or has not changed you in some way? Have you ever asked the "why" questions? Do you doubt His love for you because your circumstances tell you otherwise? I know these questions and emotional responses. Actually, even King David did, too. If you read through most of the Psalms written by him, you recognize his emotional roller coaster at times in questions such as, "Why are you downcast o my soul and why so disturbed?"

(Psalm 42:11). Yet, he was a man after God's own heart (Acts 13:22). We are not perfect, and we don't need to hide from the Lord. I tell those in counseling, "God has big shoulders; just tell Him how you feel. He wants you to come to Him." That's the main point. He just wants His children to reach out to Him.

KNOW HIS LOVE

This is the time where you need to hear how much God loves you. No, do not push that sentence away! Let it reverberate to the core of your being. When I was broken, I had a difficult time realizing how much God loved me. I thought my situation revealed a different characteristic than what the Bible stated. How could God say He loved me when I was hurt so badly?

The enemy, the devil, is the father of all lies (John 8:44). He wants you to think that God has left you, thereby triggering you to question, "If God really loved me, then why did He allow this to happen?" You may even think God is good for everyone else but you because in some way you are not good enough or special enough.

Here is the truth: John 3:16. We were dead in our own sin, and God wanted to have relationship with us so fiercely that He sent His Son, Jesus, to die on a Cross and give eternal life to those who believe. When Adam and Eve sinned in the Garden of Eden, that broke fellowship with God. They were removed from the Garden and placed outside of it. This placement prevented them from walking in His presence unhindered.

The Law was given through Moses to institute sacrifices because without the shedding of blood, there can be no forgiveness of sins (Hebrews 9:22). Jesus came in the form of a human and lived among us to reveal the Father and lay down His life as the sacrifice to pay for our debt. He rose from the dead after three days and is now seated at the Father's right hand (Ephesians 1:20). We can only love Him because He first loved us (1 John 4:19). Romans 5:6-8 says, "You see, at just the right time, when we were still powerless, Christ died for the ungodly. Very rarely will anyone die for a righteous person, though for a good person someone might possibly dare to die. But God demonstrates his own love for us in this: While we were still sinners, Christ died for us." The knowledge of Jesus as your Savior is critical to receiving His love. Let the Spirit draw you to Him right now.

Once we admit this truth, He meets us right where we are. In Romans 8:35-39, Paul emphasizes how the love of the Lord will never leave us:

> *Who shall separate us from the love of Christ? Shall trouble or hardship or persecution or famine or nakedness or danger or sword? As it is written: "For your sake we face death all day long; we are considered as sheep to be slaughtered." No, in all these things we are more than conquerors through him who loved us. For I am convinced that neither death nor life, neither angels nor demons, neither the present nor the future, nor any powers, neither height nor depth, nor anything else in all creation, will be able to separate us from the love of God that is in Christ Jesus our Lord.*

Nothing can separate you from God's love. No mistakes or decisions you made can make God angry at you and cause Him to cease loving you. No harm done to you can make you unlovable. Situations come and go, but the Lover of your soul remains. Yes, until eternity and beyond!

Why can nothing separate us from the love of God? Because He does not just love us. Love is not simply something He does. It is not only a characteristic of Him. He *is* love! 1 John 4:7-8 says, "Dear friends, let us love one another, for love comes from God. Everyone who loves has been born of God and knows God. Whoever does not love does not know God, because God is love."

The personality traits of the Lord do not change based on time, space, or circumstances. Just because human love wanes or fades over time does not mean His does. We may set requirements for people to meet in order for us to love them, but the Lord does not. Jesus remains the same today, tomorrow, and forever, so His love is forever (Hebrews 13:8).

Human love falls short at times, leaving people feeling betrayed, abandoned, and rejected. What about the quality of love offered by our Father? In Ephesians 3:17-19, the Apostle Paul writes, "And I pray that you, being rooted and established in love, may have power, together with all the Lord's holy people, to grasp how wide and long and high and deep is the love of Christ, and to know this love that surpasses knowledge—that you may be filled to the measure of all the fullness of God." We can only grasp the width, length, height, and depth of love when we remain rooted in Christ. We cannot wrap our minds around that love, either. I have tried many times to figure out how this type of love is possible, but honestly, I usually end up with a headache from thinking too much. This type of love is experiential and the reason why all the testimonies in this book have hearts on fire for the Lord. The choice to receive the love opens oneself to actually "feel" it. I will never forget during a time of fasting and prayer, I was sitting in a chair when all of a sudden I felt a warmth cover my entire being. I was so full of the love of God that I was afraid to move. I did not want that experience to end. Because of this, I often pray, "Lord help me to know your love today. Open my eyes and ears to recognize when Your love is in action."

An awareness of this love must remain at the forefront of our thoughts in order to receive the fullness of the Lord. How many times a day does a person eat? This answer will vary, but for the most part people eat multiple times a day to stay full. The concept is similar to our spiritual walk. What would happen if we felt depleted of love and went to the Lover of our soul to be filled? Can you imagine the peace and joy that would transpire? Connectedness to the love of God allows a person to continue to view Him in a true and unadulterated way. Even Jesus urged the disciples to remain in His love (John 15:9).

BE MINDFUL OF HIM

Another aspect of finding peace with God is to be mindful of Him. When a person has suffered pain from the past, the mind can be overwhelmed with the situation that the ability to keep one's eyes on Jesus becomes difficult. The mind tends to replay things in order to comprehend what is going on. Shutting the mind off from this tendency is not only necessary, but critical to heal. Unfortunately, the more time spent trying to figure things out, the deeper the wound goes within the heart.

What if you are the person who does not feel wounded but senses something within you needs to be revealed? Then keep reading. The answer you search for might come in the following paragraphs through the Spirit's illumination.

One main way to increase mindfulness of the Lord is to sit still in His presence. Psalm 46:10 says, "Be still, and know that I am God." How do we become still? Choose an easily accessible place and a time where interruptions are limited. If it is difficult to stop thoughts from entering the mind, put on worship music first and just praise the Lord. Read a psalm and pray through that. The goal is to first become centered on the Lord. Once stillness results, then invite the Lord to speak. Allow Him to reveal who He is and who you are in Him. If the mind wanders, which it will at first, gently pull it back to the now moment. Keep focused on God. If it continues to wander, begin to come up with different names or characteristics for the Lord from A to Z. Tell Him, "God, you are awesome, beautiful, compassionate, deliverer, everlasting, faithful, good, my helper," and so on.

Being still may come in spurts. Initially, five minutes may be all you can muster. As the practice expands, so too will your ability to remain longer. The amount of time will depend on your daily schedule. You may be able to sit for twenty minutes one day and only a couple of minutes another. The important part is that you try. In addition, there will be times when the Lord speaks, and other times when you hear nothing.

The most amazing aspect of this time is that peace will begin to flow. The situation may not change immediately, but your reaction to it will. Emotions will begin to level out, and your ability to withstand more emotional pain will result. During these times, God may reveal a Scripture to hold onto or put a picture of Him in your mind. He may unfold a plan of action or divulge wisdom on what not to do. Trust the Lord to know what is needed and at the right time. He will also strengthen you to handle everything going on because you can do all things through Christ who strengthens you (Philippians 4:13).

Another benefit of being still is the recognition that God is moving. Even though one cannot see all God is doing, a focus on current blessings materializes. I love the line in the song, "Waymaker," that says, "Even though I don't see it, You're moving. Even though I don't feel it, You're moving. You never stop. You never stop moving."[3] How can we be in His presence and not perceive how blessed we are? The blindedness from pain is removed, and our vision returns to the King of Kings. This, in turn, produces hope. Again, situations may not change immediately, but our perspective does.

God will not leave you or forsake you (Hebrews 13:5). Allow this truth to soak into the fibers of your being. If you have felt the fear of abandonment, the truth that God will never leave you must replace the lie that says everyone else will leave.

God says He will not fail or leave you helpless. He wants to help you. God is right there with you—when you cry yourself to sleep at night, when you get frustrated with yourself because you did that "thing" again, when you drive home from work, or when you take a walk. He is with you when someone is threatening to harm you or when someone is berating you. When you are mindful of His presence, you can repeat what the author states in Hebrews 13:6, "So we say with confidence, 'The Lord is my helper; I will not fear; what can man do to me?'"

The Scripture the Lord gave me during one of my times of being still when broken was Psalm 91. I read it multiple times a day, and it brought me such peace, knowing that the Lord would take care of me when I resided in His presence. Further, I often quoted a few lines from a song I heard at the time, "I don't live by what I feel, but by Your truth You are revealed. I'm not holding onto You, but You are holding onto me."[4] Knowing we are in the palm of God's hand is very comforting. I encourage you right now just to picture God holding your hand. Go ahead, and try it. No one is watching.

God says to come to Him, and He will give us rest (Matthew 11:28-30), but we have to be mindful of Him in order to go to Him. This rest is vital to overcoming the past. Knowing that the battle for salvation is complete and won displaces guilt and shame. Knowing that God is sovereign eliminates the need to try to figure things out. Rest brings about a deep peace that situations cannot steal. This rest brings about peace at the very depth of who we are. Our spirits rest. Our minds rest. Our bodies rest.

When we take His yoke upon us, then we allow Him to handle our present and future. We allow Him to instruct us on the direction to go and the truth of the matter. The still small voice can be heard saying, "This is the way." At times, this references physical acts, but also reflects beliefs and attitudes such as forgiveness, patience, kindness, peace, gentleness, and self-control. Basically, the fruit of the Spirit (Galatians 5:22-23).

TRUST HIM

Another major aspect of finding peace with God is learning to trust Him. Jeremiah 29:11 states, "'For I know the plans I have for you,' declares the Lord, 'plans to prosper you and not to harm you, plans to give you hope and a future.'" Woundedness often creates a view of personal insignificance, and this stance leads a person to believe that he or she does not matter. This verse brings insight to the fact that we were created for something bigger than ourselves, and that recognition remains vital for transformation.

The Lord does not want to harm His children but rather to give them hope and a future. If we trust that God has a future for us, then that must mean the pain has an end date. During intense emotional pain, people can become so wrapped up in the moment that it controls their ability to think beyond that pain, thus triggering them to believe that they have no future. How the devil makes people believe such enormous lies! All a person sees is the devil winning out. But God! We can be overcomers in Christ when we entrust the future to Him.

When circumstances bring confusion and a lack of understanding, those things have the potential to provoke doubt. Doubt, in turn, makes it difficult to place confidence in the Lord. One of the most quoted Scriptures to assist in this area is Proverbs 3:5-6, which reads, "Trust in the Lord with all your heart and lean not on your own understanding; in all your ways submit to him, and he will make your paths straight." The NIV footnote says, or 'direct your paths.'

When we let go of needing to understand, then the Lord can lead us. But if we continue to allow the inability to wrap our minds around an event, then our attention is focused on what lays behind instead of the potential which beckons us forward. If you find yourself at the place of bewilderment, pray through it. Ask the Lord to help you surrender the pain, situation, and emotions so you may see the direction He wants you to go. We are a society that wants to have all the answers. Okay, I admit, I too want to have all the answers. When the "why" escapes us, we must embrace the hand of the Lord and trust that He knows where we are going and what we need. We must grapple with the fact that God is sovereign and that trusting in Him is the best choice we can make.

God can turn all things to the good of those who love Him (Romans 8:28). Even when conditions seem bleak and irreversible, the Lord can and will bring something good from it. When my friend, Angela, lost her husband in a car accident, it was traumatic. Grief appeared overwhelming at times, yet she walked with such grace that it encouraged others to trust the Lord. Additionally, the beauty that Jesus brought from it was in the form of a ministry. My friend now comforts many others with the consolation she was given (2 Corinthians 1:4) as she leads grief groups.

The last thing you want to hear when you are at the pinnacle of emotional pain is that something good will come out of your experience. I know it does not feel as though that is even possible, but it is true. Focus on what you know, not on how you feel at this moment. If you continue to trust the Lord, He promises to turn it around. A note of caution: God is not required to meet certain expectations for what this will look like. Trust entails permitting Him to control the outcome and its timing. Once I began to quote Psalm 91, Jeremiah 29:11, and Romans 8:28 every day, my trust in the Lord began to build. Occurrences that triggered me no longer caused the same reaction because I knew God had not abandoned me and still had a plan for my life. The same is true for you.

Once salvation occurs, we need to continue to receive His love, be mindful of Him, and trust Him. Through these three avenues, true peace with God occurs. All three remain vital to obtaining transformation and continuing to live transformed. If we forfeit the love of Jesus, then it becomes much more difficult for us to trust. If we are not mindful of His presence, then negative emotions can unhinge faith.

We must pursue peace and then contend for it to remain. For we have a gracious, loving, and merciful heavenly Father. Isaiah 41:10 reminds us, "So do not fear, for I am with you; do not be dismayed, for I am your God. I will strengthen you and help you; I will uphold you with my righteous right hand." Spiritual eyes and ears must be open to recognize that the Lord is moving on our behalf. As Isaiah 26:3 declares, "You keep him in perfect peace whose mind is stayed on you, because he trusts in you." When our view of God is transformed, then our reaction to difficulties in life are also changed because we know His love and presence, and we can trust Him. This provides such peace, which promotes rest.

In order to obtain a clearer picture of how transformation unfolds from peace, grace must be explored. How is grace defined, and what does it look like in action?

CHAPTER 4

MORE THAN SALVATION

"Praise the Lord, my soul, and forget not all his benefits—who forgives all your sins and heals all your diseases, who redeems your life from the pit and crowns you with love and compassion, who satisfies your desires with good things so that your youth is renewed like the eagle's"
—Psalm 103:2-5

How wonderful to know that God loves us, and that Jesus died for us. It is amazingly freeing to consider that God forgives all sin, mistakes, and failures. When we know the love of our Father and are mindful of Him, then it increases our ability to trust Him. Although these truths are tremendous and mind blowing, the good news does not stop there.

SYD

Syd grew up in a home where her parents were close-knit with some friends. When these friends came over, they brought their children with them. These children were boys who were not good. They did unspeakable things to Syd and instructed her to just enjoy what was happening because they were sure she would like it. However, Syd did not. She showered to wash away the filth she felt and the shame that rose within her. Syd feared no one would believe her, so she was alone with her terror. The fact that her secret was kept well-hidden triggered another issue. She began to believe that being overweight would protect her from further harm because it would cause her to be unattractive. However, this only complicated the situation further.

Syd continued through life and eventually married and had two daughters. She and her husband both became ministers and pastored a church. She was the women's pastor and spoke life to others. However, inside, she was miserable, and, on the outside, she was overweight. One night their church was having a revival. She left the revival to commit suicide by driving her car into something. At about the time she was going to go through with her plan, she felt the presence of God enter her car and take over the driver's wheel. Immediately, she knew that the Lord divinely intervened and was going to transform her life.

The process that began that night was a lengthy one. Syd eventually embarked on a journey to lose the excessive weight and allow the Lord to heal all her emotional wounds. God did not take all the shame at once, but little by little, she shed pounds and pain. The Lord transformed her thinking, and spiritual disciplines assisted with the loss of weight. She lost over two hundred and sixty pounds and has maintained over one hundred and fifty pound loss and found complete freedom. Syd has turned her story into a book that has blessed many people. She continues to speak on the power of God to transform lives. She and her husband continue to pastor together. Only God can thwart our plans in order to accomplish His.

God had more for Syd than just salvation, and He does for all of us. Don't get me wrong; salvation is everything. Without it, we will *not* spend eternity in heaven. However, if we limit life to only a belief in Christ, then we are limited to an existence short of being victorious. In addition to bestowing blessings upon us, our heavenly Father wants to see His children walk in freedom and victory, like Syd. He wants to favor us when we have an intimate relationship with Him. David declares in Psalm 103 the remarkable benefits to knowing the Creator of the universe.

What are these added gains for believers? With the limited space in this book, topics include the following: continued forgiveness, grace, being an heir, assistance with fighting battles, and identifying with Christ. In order to receive these additional bonuses, one must have an ongoing relationship with the Lord. This does not mean perfection, but conversation and communion with the One who desires fellowship with His creation.

CONTINUED FORGIVENESS

The last chapter discussed salvation, but unfortunately, many people stop there. What happens when we sin or fail after we give our hearts to the Lord? I know in my life, such sin brought shame, guilt, and condemnation. Too many Christians live with these life-draining emotions. Jesus did not pay the high price of death on the Cross so you and I would be left in a pit with no way out. Yes, acceptance of Christ means our names are written in the Lamb's Book of Life. Can we still go to heaven if we live with guilt? Yes, but life will be miserable, and there is no need to live this way.

Do you feel in bondage because of your own behavior? Have you made poor decisions, and now they are coming back to haunt you? Does looking in the mirror cause too much pain? Let's turn to John 8 and the story of the woman caught in adultery. The 'important' people (Scribes and Pharisees) brought this woman to Jesus, and they wanted Him to give them permission to stone her. This was a test for Jesus, to see how He would react. I love how He responds: "When they kept on questioning him, he straightened up and said to them, 'Let any one of you who is without sin be the first to throw a stone at her'" (John 8:7). Jesus could have said, "Well you guys are right; go ahead." But instead, He responds by reminding them of their own sinfulness.

I share this Scripture to remind us that everyone falls short. Sometimes, the devil, who is the father of all lies (John 8:44) tries to tell us that we are the only ones who mess up—that we are just not good enough and never will measure up. Yet Paul reminds us that "all have sinned and fall short of the glory of God" (Romans 3:23). Jesus continues in John 8:11, "'Then neither do I condemn you,' Jesus declared. 'Go now and leave your life of sin.'" When we sin, we need to repent and move on. Even though you may have brought the situation on yourself, if you receive the continued forgiveness of Christ, God can and will bring restoration in your life. This does not mean everything will turn out the way you want, but it does mean He is with you. God even used murderers (Moses and David), an adulterer (David), tax collectors—who were the outcasts—(Matthew and Zacchaeus), and a prostitute (Rehab). If He can use them, He can use you.

At times, the most difficult circumstance is when others do not forgive you, reminding you of what you have done. First, you need to make sure you have truly apologized and asked for their forgiveness. The attitude of "They know I'm sorry" does not work as a formal apology. Take responsibility and truly repent. When that has occurred, make sure you do not repeat the behavior. Do everything in your ability to not reengage in that sin. Then, continue to embrace the blood of Jesus. There is nothing else you can do but remain humble every day and allow healing to unfold in the heart of the one you hurt.

People who are not believers, and unfortunately some Christians, may not understand what true forgiveness entails. If this is the case, humility is in order. Instead of fighting with them, do not engage. Quietly walk away. I love the response of Jesus in the story about Jairus's daughter when the servants tell him to no longer bother Jesus because she had died: "Overhearing what they said, Jesus told him, 'Don't be afraid; just believe'" (Mark 5:36). In the NIV, "overhearing" also means ignoring what they said. This is imperative to receiving forgiveness when others attempt to remind you how horrible you are. When you hear what they say, ignore it, walk away, and just believe that Christ has *already* forgiven you.

Do not allow the enemy to tell you that your sin is unforgiveable. Remember in the last chapter, we said that nothing can separate you from the love of God! Paul reminds us that "there is now no condemnation for those who are in Christ Jesus" (Romans 8:1). This brings relief. We no longer need to beat ourselves up when we fall. Our sins are washed away. In addition, when we see spiritual progress and past behaviors do not return, then the persistence of condemnation decreases.

God will not and cannot hold your sins against you once you confess them and ask for His forgiveness. God is not mad at you! He does not *give* you what you deserve, and He is not punishing you now for your sins of the past. That is not who He is. You can change. God has rescued you already from the pit. Just reach out your hand and allow Him to pull you up out of the miry clay (Psalm 40:2).

Allow the following verses to solidify in your heart the goodness of God's grace and forgiveness. David continues in Psalm 103:9-12,

> *He will not always accuse, nor will he harbor his anger forever; he does not treat us as our sins deserve or repay us according to our iniquities. For as high as the heavens are above the earth, so great is his love for those who fear him; as far as the east is from the west, so far has he removed our transgressions from us.*

Your sins are as far as the east is from the west. Will New York City and San Diego ever be side by side? No. That thought is ludicrous. So, embrace this object lesson, and apply it to your life. Your sins are covered by the blood of Jesus and removed from your life. Cease bringing them up and do not give them power over your future.

How do you learn to accept this grace-filled forgiveness? Assuming you have truly repented and no longer repeat that sin, ask—and continue to ask—the Lord to help you. Read every Scripture on forgiveness. Press into the truth of God's Word. Whenever thoughts of self-condemnation enter your thinking, refuse to think on them. Instead, meditate on the love of Jesus. Concentrate on the continued benefit of God's grace, love, and forgiveness. I proclaim Acts 13:38 over your life: "Therefore, my friends, I want you to know that through Jesus the forgiveness of sins is proclaimed to you."

GRACE

So, what is grace? In the Old Testament, grace referred to favor, compassion, mercy, and kindness. This took place both with (1) people and the Lord as well as (2) people with others who were more powerful than they were. Examples of those who had favor with God include Noah, Moses, and the Israelites. Examples of finding grace with people include Ruth with Boaz, David with Jonathan, and Esther with the king. For you and me, this means God will provide mercy and compassion when we are suffering. He can also grant favor when applying for a job or making a deal.

Have you ever wondered how you of all people obtained a certain job or promotion—or how a situation that could have been worse suddenly worked itself out? This is the grace of God. Unmerited favor. Grace is something we cannot earn. It is freely given by the Lord alone when we are in relationship with Him. We often see this when parents coach their own children in a sport. Their child tends to get to play more often or have the coveted spots on the field. They also tend to be the star player everyone wants to be like. This analogy can reflect our relationship with the Lord. Gentiles were grafted in to provoke the Jewish people to jealousy, so they too would turn to the Lord (Romans 11:11-31). Thus, we are provided grace defined as mercy, kindness, and favor in order for others to see and want what we have. When we walk in the grace of God, others witness it. I love shopping for something when there is only one left of an item, and it is on sale. This is the grace of God—His favor to bless me. I do not deserve it, yet it occurs because of His great love and kindness.

Grace in the New Testament shifts to include salvation and spiritual gifts. Salvation has already been identified in a previous chapter, but spiritual gifts are also identified as grace. The Greek term charisma means "gift of grace" as found in 1 Peter 4:10: "Each of you should use whatever gift you have received to serve others, as faithful stewards of God's grace in its various forms." What are these gifts? Romans 12:3-8 states,

> *"For by the grace given me I say to every one of you: Do not think of yourself more highly than you ought, but rather think of yourself with sober judgment, in accordance with the faith God has distributed to each of you. For just as each of us has one body with many members, and these members do not all have the same function, so in Christ we, though many, form one body, and each member belongs to all the others. We have different gifts, according to the grace given to each of us. If your gift is prophesying, then prophesy in accordance with your faith; if it is serving, then serve; if it is teaching, then teach; if it is to encourage, then give encouragement; if it is giving, then give generously; if it is to lead, do it diligently; if it is to show mercy, do it cheerfully.*

2 Corinthians 12:4-11 depicts the gifts thus:

> *"There are different kinds of gifts, but the same Spirit distributes them. There are different kinds of service, but the same Lord. There are different kinds of working, but in all of them and in everyone it is the same God at work. Now to each one the manifestation of the Spirit is given for the common good. To one there is given through the Spirit a message of wisdom, to another a message of knowledge by means of the same Spirit, to another faith by the same Spirit, to another gifts of healing by that one Spirit, to another miraculous powers, to another prophecy, to*

another distinguishing between spirits, to another speaking in different kinds of tongues, and to still another the interpretation of tongues. All these are the work of one and the same Spirit, and he distributes them to each one, just as he determines."

How amazing that God has designed each of us to have a purpose. We are not put on this earth just to take up space but to participate in making Jesus known. When I felt like such a failure, I thought God could no longer use me for ministry. I thought all my God-given dreams were over. Yet, God's gifts and calling are irrevocable (Romans 11:29). Your life is not over. You have not sinned so much that God can no longer use you. A person cannot destroy what the Lord has already placed inside of him or her. You are not damaged beyond repair. We all want to feel useful and participate in something larger than ourselves. Grace is that accomplishment. It is all about God's beautiful, masterful, and powerful plan of grace.

BEING AN HEIR

What does it mean to be an heir? *Merriam-Webster* states three different meanings. First, an heir is "one who receives property from an ancestor: one who is entitled to inherit property."[5] Second, an heir is "one who inherits or is entitled to succeed to a hereditary rank, title, or office."[6] Last, "one who receives or is entitled to receive something other than property from a parent or predecessor."[7] So to sum up the definition, an heir is a person who is *entitled* to inherit—from a parent or someone who died before them—property, rank, title, or office which is now bestowed upon them. Wow. When we look at this all-inclusive understanding, being an heir is pretty powerful.

First, regarding the entitlement and identification as a child in order to inherit, John 1:12 declares, "Yet to all who did receive him, to those who believed in his name, he gave the right to become children of God." If you believe in Jesus, then you have become a child of God.

What does being a child of the Most High warrant? There are tremendous advantages of having a famous parent (most people know Him), who is extravagant (His love and goodness are endless), and who is wealthy (He owns the cattle on a thousand hills). Healthy parents want their children to succeed, thrive, and be victorious. There is such joy in watching one's child experience and embrace life. Parents will also stop at nothing to protect, teach, and provide for every need. Now, if earthly parents desire to build up, surround, and launch their children out into the world, how much more the God of all creation?

What happens when your earthly parents were unhealthy, nonexistent, or abandoned you? I love what God's word says in Psalm 27:10, "Though my father and mother forsake me, the Lord will receive me." Another translation says that God has adopted us as His own. So even though your childhood may have been riddled with pain, fear, anger, or heartache, once you become a child of God, then He takes over as Father.

Before we get too far into what it means to be a child of God, it is important to lay the foundation as to why the Creator of the universe wanted us. Ephesians 1:4-5 reveals, "For he chose us in him before the creation of the world to be holy and blameless in his sight. In love he predestined us for adoption to sonship through Jesus Christ, in accordance with his pleasure and will." God thought about a relationship with you and me before He even spoke the land and water into existence out of love. He wanted to share with humans what was created, and it pleased Him to do so. You are not an afterthought or a mistake. You were planned by your Father with precision for just this moment in time. The year you were born was the exact year God had created, called, and anointed you to accomplish His purposes.

Moving along. If your child (or, for those who don't have children—perhaps a niece or nephew) asked for bread to eat, would you give him or her a lemon? No, you would not. So, if you are open and willing to give your child good things, how much more does your heavenly Father want to give you *every* good and perfect gift (Matthew 7:11). We just need to ask the Lord. In multiple Scriptures Jesus instructs us to pray according to His will and ask in His name, and it shall be granted (Matthew 21:22; John 14:13-14; 1 John 5:14). Don't you think that if you prayed for strength that He would grant it? Or if you prayed for wisdom from the God who gives abundantly, wouldn't He without fault provide revelation and insight (James 1:5)?

When was the last time you truly asked your Father to help you overcome the pain you feel? Have you given up on prayer because you feel as though nothing has changed? Do you feel unworthy to ask? Press into prayer! Do not remain silent; instead, continue to cry out to the Lord. He will answer. The parable of the unjust judge who grants the widow's request because she continued to go before him and plead her case reminds each one of us that if a human person would respond this way, how much more will the Creator of the universe, our Daddy, want to reach out (Luke 18:1-8)?

Jesus came to earth in human form to sacrifice His life for us. This has already been established. But what benefit does that act bring to us? Jesus serves as our High Priest who has suffered and was tempted just like we have been. He can protect us and teach us because He knows exactly what we are going through (Hebrews 4:15). As a parent, when you watch your children suffer, don't you wish you could take it all away for them? So does your Father. This is why He gives us a playground with a fence to keep us from going outside His will. The Bible instructs us so we do not fall away from Him into situations we will later regret. This is true love. Have you ever said to your child, "This hurts me more than it does you?" I never believed it when my parents said that to me, but wow, how true that statement actually was. I have repeated it to my nieces and nephew.

Another area of generosity is that our Father wants to meet our every need. Needs and wants are two different things. Too many people confuse the two, and they become discouraged when their want is not met. Honestly, when a person feels overwhelmed emotionally, that skews their ability to discern the difference between needs and wants. But God does desire to provide for you. His Word says in Philippians 4:19, "And my God will meet all your needs according to the riches of his glory in Christ Jesus." This means your need for protection, met; your need for stability, met; your need for finances, met; your need for wisdom, met; and your need for direction, met. I think you get my point. Furthermore, since we have a High Priest who understands, we can boldly draw near to His throne of grace and find help in our time of trouble (Hebrews 4:16).

These are tremendous blessings for us as children to enjoy. But let's go further into becoming heirs. What happens when a parent dies? Romans 8:15-18 declares,

The Spirit you received does not make you slaves, so that you live in fear again; rather, the Spirit you received brought about your

adoption to sonship. And by him we cry, "Abba, Father." The Spirit himself testifies with our spirit that we are God's children. Now if we are children, then we are heirs—heirs of God and co-heirs with Christ, if indeed we share in his sufferings in order that we may also share in his glory.

There are many lessons in this one Scripture, but I want to focus on the heir section. The Greek meaning of the phrase "adoption to sonship" refers to the full legal standing of an adopted male heir in Roman culture. Listeners at the time of the writing of these verses would have understood the term utilized here. We today know what legalities are afforded to an heir. If you are a child of God, then you are an heir. There is no question left to challenge. You belong—period. I pray you no longer tolerate the enemy's lies that you are unloved or unwanted.

Furthermore, in order to be an heir, someone must have died. That someone is Christ. When He died on the Cross, He bestowed to every person who calls upon His name the right to what He possessed at the time. What did Jesus leave us? He bestowed on us the Holy Spirit, power, authority, healing, and the right to come before His Father and ask in His name that every need be met.

Prior to Jesus ascending into heaven, He instructed the disciples to go to Jerusalem and wait for the power from on high—the promised Holy Spirit (Acts 1:4-5). Jesus said the Spirit would be granted to us to remind us of what He said, to lead us into all truth, and to be our comforter, helper, advocate, intercessor, counselor, strengthener, and standby (John 14:26, AMP). We have all the rescuing we need in the Spirit. He is ready and able to intervene on our behalf. Now that is a gift I want as an heir! The same Spirit who raised Jesus from the dead lives in us. We must lean into Him in order to inherit this assistance. I pray that dead marriages, failing businesses, and faltering ministries will awaken right now in the name of Jesus!

Power and authority go hand in hand. Jesus had bestowed it on His disciples when He instructed them to deliver people and heal them (Matthew 10:1; Luke 9:1). Acts reveals this power and authority throughout the birth of the Church, and that power remains relevant for us today. We have the ability to defeat darkness with the Light and the authority to speak to mountains that they must be removed (Mark 11:23). What is the hindrance in our lives? We must embrace this power and authority as heirs. We cannot sit on the sidelines and believe the lie that we stand helpless and hopeless. Without putting this benefit of being an heir into practice, it remains useless.

Last, healing is transferred through heirship. Healing is not just physical, but spiritual, emotional, and mental as well. We are reassured of this when Isaiah prophesies in 53:4-5 that Jesus took our pain and bore our suffering so that by the wounds on His body we are healed and made whole. What you struggle with right now, God can heal. Blinding depression, addiction, betrayal, grief, anger, or any other negative emotion has the potential for healing and freedom when brought to the Cross. This is an earth-shattering accomplishment available to us as heirs.

God has given us the title of heir. We are of the rank and office of priesthood in a priestly kingdom (1 Peter 2:9; Revelation 5:10). However, none of these qualities mentioned above is worth much unless we introduce them into our pain and brokenness. They must be established in our lives to reap the benefit.

ASSISTANCE WITH FIGHTING BATTLES

In 2 Chronicles 20 when King Jehoshaphat saw that a multitude of people were coming against him, he could have gone into hiding. He could have come up with a battle plan all on his own. But how did he respond as a believer in the Great I Am? He ran to the Lord! Not only did he turn wholeheartedly to God, but he instructed all the people to fast and pray with him (2 Chronicles 20:3). How did God the Protector respond? 2 Chronicles 20:14-17 shows:

> *"Then the Spirit of the Lord came on Jahaziel son of Zechariah, the son of Benaiah, the son of Jeiel, the son of Mattaniah, a Levite and descendant of Asaph, as he stood in the assembly. He said: 'Listen, King Jehoshaphat and all who live in Judah and Jerusalem! This is what the Lord says to you: 'Do not be afraid or discouraged because of this vast army. For the battle is not yours, but God's. Tomorrow march down against them. They will be climbing up by the Pass of Ziz, and you will find them at the end of the gorge in the Desert of Jeruel. You will not have to fight this battle. Take up your positions; stand firm and see the deliverance the Lord will give you, Judah and Jerusalem. Do not be afraid; do not be discouraged. Go out to face them tomorrow, and the Lord will be with you.'"*

The Lord responded by declaring that He would fight the battle. All the Israelites had to do was take up their positions, stand straight, and watch God work. He wanted them to stand in faith and not fear, so He reminded them that they were not alone. How awesome to receive this response when not knowing what to do.

See, the Lord wants each of us to know that one benefit of believing in Him is that we do not have to figure things out but rather do what He instructs, and He will fight for us. How many times do we engage in conflict when it was never meant for us to tackle alone? Honestly, I know I could have avoided some situations altogether if I just would have followed King Jehoshaphat's lead. Sometimes, we complicate matters more than was ever intended. I remember a time when I was so stressed out from the church plant closing that I was physically sick. As I leaned over the toilet and vomited, I heard the Spirit speak to me and say, "It doesn't have to be like this. Get up and walk in My strength." Instantly, I stood up and no longer felt nauseous. A song came into my mind, which I discussed in chapter 2 of this book, that says I don't live by how I feel. All day I quoted that song and Psalm 91:1 where it states that those who live in the shadow of the Almighty shall remain stable and fixed (AMP). I reminded myself that I was stable and fixed in Jesus. I continued to place one foot in front of the other, worked all day, and never felt that stressed out or anxious again during that time.

How did the situation turn out with King Jehoshaphat? The Lord fought the battle and won mightily. Because of this, the fear of God came upon all the kingdoms around them, and the Israelites had peace (2 Chronicles 20:29-30). Oh friends, if we would just allow the Lord to fight our battles, peace would exist as the prominent outcome. God can do the same for you. Turn to Him, and ask Him to take over for you so you can rest. When God is on your side, He provides direction, wisdom, and strength. The terms of the battle are the Lord's alone. Just be still and know He is God (Psalm 46:10).

The part in between the prayer and the outcome is imperative to identify. What did the Israelites do as they waited for the breakthrough to come? They praised and worshipped the Lord

(2 Chronicles 20:18-29). The pressure was off them to figure everything out and implement a specific plan on their own. They knew who was in their corner, which brought peace and rest. Zechariah 4:6 declares, "'Not by might, nor by power, but by my Spirit,' says the Lord Almighty." Additionally, when we recognize who the battle is really against—Satan, then we learn that people are not the problem. Yes, the enemy works through people, but they are not our foe. More information pertaining to battles will be addressed in a separate chapter devoted solely to the battleground.

IDENTIFYING WITH CHRIST

The last aspect of this chapter is learning to identify with Christ. We must acknowledge what Jesus gave up when He came to earth. He stripped himself of His heavenly nature and came to earth to die a horrible death (Philippians 2:6-8). I find it easier to identify with someone who knows what I am going through than someone who gives 'Christianese' answers to pain. Scripture does not share much about the childhood of Jesus, but we do receive a clear look at the suffering on our behalf. What existed as a benefit for us meant pain for Him. Jesus was rejected by the ones He came to save, was betrayed by family and even a disciple, was misunderstood by the masses, and was tortured. Yet, we too will have trials and tribulations (Matthew 16:33) because those who hated Jesus will hate us (John 15:18-27).

The Spirit led our Savior out into the wilderness to be tempted and tried (Matthew 4:1). If Jesus was not spared from this, we will not be either. Before His public ministry, He had to conquer Satan's schemes. While times of testing or stretching are difficult and can be painful, they produce great fruit. Jesus taught the disciples that when they stay connected to Him, they would produce lasting results (John 15:1-15). The greatest benefit is sharing with others the glory of the Lord. While no discipline, testing, or trial feel comfortable, we can then pass onto others what we received in our time of need. Paul says we are positioned to provide comfort for others (2 Corinthians 1:4).

Jesus even told us that we will do greater things than He did—to heal, deliver, minister to, and encourage others (John 14:12-14). Do you want to do great things for the Lord? I know I want as many people to know about Him as possible. In order for this to occur, as John the Baptist writes, "He must increase, but I must decrease" (John 3:30). The only way I know for this to transpire is if I die to self. This process can be hard, though. When we learn that it is not all about us, then and only then can we begin to truly live free. There is nothing more powerful than a believer in Christ who exhibits this freedom where the Spirit of God overflows and impacts all those who come into contact with the person. Brokenness is the only way to experience this depth, thus making our trials and suffering an overall benefit.

Oh, how marvelous to believe in the Alpha and Omega, King of kings, and Lord of lords. There is no greater privilege than to be counted as a child of God whose name is written in the Lamb's Book of Life. Begin to invite the Spirit now to remind you daily of these benefits. Speak them out, and reread this chapter as often as needed. It is the truth that sets you free. These truths are life-altering if we set our minds on them. Keep your eyes on Jesus—by renewing your mind daily.

CHAPTER 5

LIFE IN THE WORD

"The thief comes only to steal and kill and destroy;
I have come that they may have life and have it to the full"
—John 10:10

In the above Scripture, we see two forces that wage war —the enemy and Jesus. The enemy attempts to steal our joy, kill our dreams, and destroy our lives. There is nothing, and I repeat—nothing—good in the enemy. There is only heartache and death. Darkness envelops those who do not know the Savior. On the other hand, Christ came so we may have fullness of life, which brings peace, hope, and energy. Light surrounds those walking in relationship with the Lord. Can you sense the dichotomy between darkness and light? Does the pressure of the pull in one direction or the other overwhelm you at times? How do we overcome evil and walk in victory? We must turn to the Word of God, dig deep, and abide in Him.

JANA

Jana grew up in a home with parents who were functioning addicts. On the outside, her family seemed normal. Yet keeping the family secret caused Jana tremendous anxiety and depression, which triggered suicidal thoughts around the age of seven. At first, she isolated herself in order to cope but then realized that if she tried to be like others, then she might be accepted. This began a journey down the road of alcohol and drug use to cover pain and to fill a void.

Jana had her first child at the age of fourteen, which caused her to grow up quickly. She turned her life around to become a mother. Eventually, though, when her son was a little older and she had family around to watch him, she began to party again. She tried to find her worth in men and got married when she was eighteen, but that marriage only lasted six years. One year later, she met her second husband and began using cocaine, methamphetamines, and drinking alcohol. Excitement resulted with this new relationship but quickly dwindled. Jana did not really want to be clean but became sober for her children, only to realize later it was God drawing her to Him. Her second husband overdosed on heroin, which brought about even more pain for her and her four children.

Jana met another man whom she married, and they began attending church. They both gave their hearts to the Lord, and Jana realized that God was the only answer to all her pain. She dove into the Word of God and was able to forgive her parents and release resentment and bitterness. Her worth was now determined by the Lord and not what others did to her or what she said to herself. Freedom came from the Lord alone. Jana did not receive any formal help or counseling, mainly due to the shame she carried and the fear of judgment from others. The more she learned and read the Bible, the hungrier she became to know more. The weight of the world was gone, and a passion to help rescue others resulted. Jana had found freedom, and her view of self was transformed into who God had created her to be. Jana now co-leads a Celebrate Recovery group at church to bring the hope of freedom to many others. She also worked as a case manager assisting those with addiction issues to obtain treatment when they presented to an emergency room. This journey has led Jana and her husband Joe to foster children to help them and their families break free from the bondage of abuse, neglect, and addiction. They have even adopted one daughter whose biological parents were addicts. Once again, only the truth of who God is and who she was in Him brought transformation. Even when she found sobriety without the Lord, true freedom only resulted when Jesus entered the picture and His Word brought life.

In John 14:6, Jesus says that He is the way, the truth, and the life. He describes here the ability for each of us to have an eternal and daily perspective. This perspective is not only universal, but personal. Jesus is not merely saying He *knows* the way, but that He *is* the Way. His truth is not one of many, but He is the *only* Truth. Jana discovered He is the answer to every earthly problem she encountered as she journeyed through life with Him, we can too. When we have had a trial or are broken, we do not feel alive. We may go through times of numbness or feel dead inside, but that is not God's best for us. As a matter of fact, it is *opposite* of what Jesus came to earth to accomplish. No matter our circumstances, we still have the ability for life.

The previous chapter in this book identified the benefits of believing in Christ. Let us go even deeper. Once we know the goodness, love, and grace of our Lord, we can live daily in His life.

WE MUST FIRST LAY A FOUNDATION

Understanding the Relationship of the Written Word and the Living Word

John 1:1-5 states, "In the beginning was the Word, and the Word was with God, and the Word was God. He was with God in the beginning. Through him all things were made; without him nothing was made that has been made. In him was life, and that life was the light of all mankind. The light shines in the darkness, and the darkness has not overcome it." How powerful this Scripture is to all of creation! The Word has always existed. The Word is God. "Word" here in the Greek is *logos*. It is defined as the spoken word with emphasis on the meaning attempted to be conveyed; so therefore it is an expression of "personality in communication."[8] Thus, the Word is a distinct person, apart from God, yet being one with Him. The Word was *with* God, which denotes unity in creation and being face-to-face with Him. There is an equality and yet a distinction.

But who exactly is the Word, and what is His personality? John 1:14 says, "The Word became flesh and made his dwelling among us. We have seen his glory, the glory of the one and only Son, who came from the Father, full of grace and truth." Jesus is the Word made flesh. The Word lived among us.

The term *became* in John 1:14 implies a change of being. The Word left heaven and dwelt among us. This concept of dwelling means to pitch a tent and actually live day to day on earth. What picture comes to your mind? For me, I see a person who purchases the house next door and becomes my neighbor. Who is this Word made flesh? Jesus. He alone is the Son of God who left heaven and came to save us. He alone is full of grace and truth.

Merrill Tenney in his commentary on the book of John in describing *logos* says, "John uses this term to indicate that Jesus is [a] universal rather than a local significance and that he spoke with ultimate authority. He was preexistent, involved in the act of creation, and therefore superior to all created beings. This presentation lifts Christ above the materialistic."[9] Since the Word is elevated above earthly confines, then no circumstance can overcome, nullify, or erase Him. Jesus said that heaven and earth will end, yet His words will last forever (Mark 13:31). The Word brings life to all who embrace Him. He shines all around, and no plan of the devil has been able to stop His impact, nor will the enemy ever be able to. When Jesus is accepted and embraced, the *logos* comes to live inside of us. This power is above all worldly manifestations.

The Authority of Scripture

Why then do so many people still not read, study, and live out the Bible? Some people have made statements like, "The Bible is outdated," or "I pick and choose what is relevant for my life." Sometimes the demands of life squelch the desire and time available to devote to reading Scripture. To live transformed, a hunger and commitment to the Word remains vital. The Word of God here does not refer to the incarnation of Christ, but any word that God utters. But can it be completely trusted?

Second Timothy 3:16 proclaims, "All scripture is God-breathed and is useful for teaching, rebuking, correcting and training in righteousness." Every chapter and verse included in the biblical canon has a purpose, and Scripture interprets Scripture. What do I mean by this? We do not get to choose one Scripture and base a whole belief system on what it says. Each verse supports and ties into others. Context must also be considered as well as original intent. When one does not invest time truly learning the meaning and purpose of a specific verse, then one may turn or twist that verse to fit what he or she wants the passage to say. This approach does not bring life but deception. This is the main reason I devote a whole chapter to this topic.

You can trust that every Scripture comes from the throne room and heart of God through the Spirit and out of the ink of a writing utensil.

Yet some people challenge the validity of the Bible because there are multiple translations. Why are there different versions of the Bible? To attempt to give an easy answer is daunting, but here is a short summary. First, the original language of the Old Testament was Hebrew and Greek in the New Testament. From there, Scripture was translated into other languages throughout the centuries and finally into English. Exact word for word use has limitations. Then, there has been a transition of English verbiage over the years. New translations have been added to simplify the meaning and make it more understandable using more modern language.

Additionally, it also depends on the translator's motive. Let me explain. Some translators want to convey an exact word-for-word literal focus. This is referred to as formal equivalence, such as the KJV, ESV, and NASB. Other people want to transmit a thought-for-thought process, which makes it easier to read for most people. This is referred to as functional equivalence and includes the NLT, NIV and Amplified. Finally, there are individuals who want to incorporate both word-by-word and thought-by-thought in a balanced way to bring about the closest translation yet retain a version that is easier to understand. This is optimal equivalence and includes the HCSB.

Why are some verses missing from a few versions, such as Mark 16:9-20; John 5:4; and Acts 8:37? The newer translations are not removing Scripture but usually place those verses in the footnotes. Why do they do this? Scholars believe the missing Scriptures were not part of the original manuscripts. It is believed that scribes added notations to help understand the story and over the years, a few of these were added into the printed Bible. These added verses do not alter the meaning and are of minor significance. The question of a few missing verses does not undo the main message of salvation through the cross. The Holy Spirit has preserved the written Word of God for years in order to safeguard it for generations to come. Do not allow the enemy to sway you to throw away all Scripture because of notes added to aid with comprehension.

My goal in addressing these issues briefly is to increase your trust in the Bible. When the enemy can cause confusion and trigger doubt, then a person's ability to receive truth is hindered. When a Scripture is meant to bring correction, it becomes powerless to alter actions when there is opportunity to rationalize the irrelevancy. If people do not know that *every* Scripture is God-breathed, then they will pick and choose texts to suit their lifestyle. This does not bring life to a person but the need to continue to justify his or her actions.

You must solidify in your mind that scriptures in our Bibles today are meant to be there. If one is missing from your translation, then understand the reasoning presented for why, and move on. Do not become hung up on it. Furthermore, do not entertain the lie that mere men wrote what they wanted, but were moved along by the Spirit. Times might be different than the original setting, but God remains the same. His truth has endured though kingdoms, governments, and technological changes.

The Power of Scripture

Now that the authority of Scripture has been established, it is time to contemplate the power that resides in it. Hebrews 4:12 declares, "For the word of God is alive and active. Sharper than any double-edged sword, it penetrates even to dividing soul and spirit, joints and marrow; it judges the thoughts and attitudes of the heart." The Word of God here does not refer to the incarnation of Christ, but any word that God utters as evidenced by the analogy of a sword penetrating the human soul. The descriptors of "alive" and "active" reveal that there is a dynamic power at work within us when God's Word pierces us. Leon Morris in his commentary on Hebrews clarifies this verse:

> What the author is saying is that God's Word can reach to the innermost recesses of our being. We must not think that we can bluff our way out of anything, for there are no secrets hidden from God. We cannot keep our thoughts to ourselves... The Word of God passes judgement on men's feelings and on their thoughts. Nothing evades the scope of this Word. What man holds as most secret he finds subject to its scrutiny and judgement.[10]

Nothing remains hidden from the Lord. When we allow the Word to penetrate our lives, healing is possible. Freedom results.

We are delivered from lies, blinders, and skeletons in our closet, just like Jana was. So why not begin to open your heart right now? Stop reading and just invite the Holy Spirit into the deepest part of you. He already knows everything about you, anyway, so why not accept this truth and determine that you are no longer remaining where you are? It is time for *change!*

God's Word is alive! Do you need new life right now? Do you need to be revived? The way to obtain such reviving is to read the Bible. The words on the page will penetrate your heart if you allow them to. Sometimes reading the Word will feel uplifting, and other times you will recognize the need to alter behaviors because sometimes the Word is meant to correct. Ouch! However, every word is powerful—even if portions are difficult to read—because ultimately the Word brings life. The author of Hebrews reminds us that no discipline feels good in the moment, but it produces lasting results if we allow it to train us (Hebrews 12:11).

In John 8, Jesus informs His disciples that if they hold to His teaching, they really are His disciples indeed, and He goes on to say that then they will know the truth and be set free (vv. 31-32). The people, claiming heirship with Abraham to avoid being enslaved, miss the whole point. Jesus continues by revealing that all who sin are a slave, but that He came to set them free. "And if the Son sets them free, then they are free indeed" (John 8:33-36). It is the truth of the risen Christ and His Word alone that sets us free. No matter what we attempt to tell ourselves to find ease from the conviction of sin, it will never provide the peace for which we long. Additionally, we find freedom from earthly pressures when we apply Scripture to our fallen thinking and situations.

Psalm 119:50 in the Amplified Bible declares, "This is my comfort in my affliction, that Your word has revived me and given me life." I love this verse. It provides much needed hope in times of suffering. Only through God's Word does new life prevail. What is the best way to be revived? Find time to read the Bible every day. All the lives written about in chapter 2 of this book were only transformed when they took the time to immerse themselves into Scripture. This is a process and not a done-in-one-time sitting. People must make a conscious choice to nurture the spiritual discipline of reading the Bible regularly.

How can we be even more confident that transformation is possible through reading the Word of God? The Lord's response to Jeremiah reassures us, "For I am watching to see that my word is fulfilled" (Jeremiah 1:12). God is always watching. God also tells Isaiah,

As the rain and the snow come down from heaven, and do not return to it without watering the earth and making it bud and flourish, so that it yields seed for the sower and bread for the eater, so is my word that goes out from my mouth; it will not return to me empty, but will accomplish what I desire and achieve the purpose for which I sent it. —Jeremiah 55:10-11

Oh, how these two Scriptures bring courage to believe for a better tomorrow! A certain resolve sets in when we begin to ingest this truth. If God watches His Word to make sure it is fulfilled, and again repeats that His Word will accomplish that for which He sent it, then who are we to doubt? Can we humans undo what God solidifies? Yes and no. Yes, from the perspective that we must embrace and internalize this Word. No, from the aspect that His Word never changes. The Word does not lose its power just because we do not exercise our ability to receive it.

Moses, Joshua, and the Israelites went through turbulent times. Picture all the plagues that they either endured or witnessed. The rush to leave the familiar into the unknown I am sure triggered some fear and worry, and after they'd left Egypt, they even asked Moses if he brought them out into the wilderness to die instead of sitting around eating an abundance of food in bondage (Exodus 16:3). Then, not having water, a trial with snakes, more people dying, and then never seeing the leader Moses again. Now I call those problems! Can you imagine walking around in a desert for forty years when the journey was actually only an eleven-day trip? The frustration alone would have me reeling! Yet, I love what Joshua 21:45 reminds us, "Not one of all the Lord's good promises to Israel failed; every one was fulfilled." Boom! Not one. *All* of them were perfected. Even though we are not perfect, God is. He does not fail even when we or those around us do. His Word remains powerful, alive, and transactional.

When we repeat these Scriptures and place them all around us on sticky notes, computer screens, or our phone, then our minds are renewed.

RENEW YOUR MIND

When going through difficult times, it is imperative to keep our thoughts and eyes on Jesus. Paul reminds us that we should not worry or become anxious but pray and then keep our thoughts focused on what is true, pure, lovely, noble, or praiseworthy (Philippians 4:6-8). But how do we do this day in and day out?

Paul also reminds us not to conform to the world by acting like them but to be transformed by the renewing of our minds so we can know what God's will is for us (Romans 12:2). Reading the Bible not only brings life but changes the way we think. Why is this important? When our minds are renewed and focused on Jesus, we can think more clearly. We can utilize wisdom more and discern what steps we might need to take. But it goes much deeper than this. When we are reminded who God is and who we are in Him, strength builds, peace resumes, and joy surfaces. Sometimes we get so caught up in what we are supposed to be doing that we forget to just sit still at His feet. We become more like Martha by overemphasizing our work instead of like Mary, reflecting and resting in His presence (Luke 10:38-42).

When my thoughts turn negative or fearful, the minute I pick up the Bible and begin to read, I sense the nearness of the Lord, and I begin to take my eyes off the problem in front of me. I see my beloved Savior. The lies the enemy had been attempting to make me believe such as "This problem is too big, what if it this doesn't work?, what if I don't measure up?, or what if God does not come through?" are pushed out with the promises of God's omnipresence (His ability to be everywhere at the same time), omniscience (knowing all things), and omnipotence (being all powerful). I turn from feeling as though I need to figure everything out to resting in His plan and timing. How about you? Have you had an experience when your emotional state was high, but you began to read Scripture, and your thought pattern changed? If yes, reminisce on that right now. If not, keep reading—because you will!

Deuteronomy 11:18 encourages us, "Fix these words of mine in your hearts and minds; tie them as symbols on your hands and bind them on your foreheads." We are instructed to fix these words. What words is the writer referring to? In prior verses, the author was telling the Israelites to faithfully obey the commands, specifically—to love the Lord and serve Him with their whole heart and soul (Deuteronomy 11:13). When we love the Lord and serve Him, then we walk in His ways, which really is His Word. Have you ever travelled to Israel and saw traditional Jewish people with little boxes on their forehead? These are *tefillin*, small boxes that contain Scripture verses on parchment. I have seen these, and they remind me that I need to 'fix' God's Word on my heart and in my thoughts.

Deuteronomy 11:13-18 tells us why keeping God's Word in our hearts and minds is life giving. Then the Lord will send the needed rain to water the crop and the grass to feed the cattle. But if we do not fasten God's Word to ourselves, then we are likely to turn away from Him and serve other gods (earthy things), and the rain will disappear. Self-reflection time: when you are fully engaged in relationship with your Father, do you sense more of His goodness, strength, and peace regardless of your circumstances? What happens when the hours evaporate, your schedule dictates life, and it is time to coach the Little League team, play a sport, or lead that company, and you have not even had time to remind yourself who you are in Christ or who He is? Okay, one day is not going to harm anything, is it? How about five days with no devotion? Does that length of time begin to deteriorate peace, patience, or the need to control things around us? I remember interviewing Roy (see chapter 7), and he shared that he must spend every morning in the Word in order to focus on God and keep his confidence and security in Him.

What happens when you have spent time in the Word, yet as the day wears on, negative emotions and thoughts return? Jesus sent the Spirit to us to remind us what He spoke (John 14:26). Jesus said the Advocate—our counselor, helper, strengthener, and intercessor—would be right there with us. In that moment of feeling overwhelmed, angry, fearful, or depressed call out to the Lord and ask to be reminded of His promises.

Sometimes we read the Word and then quickly forget what we read. One morning I woke up with 2 Timothy 1:7 on my heart. You know the one that says, "God has not given us a spirit of fear but of power, love, and a sound mind." I thought, "Well, this is a good verse," but I did not feel afraid at that moment, so I moved on about my morning and did not reflect on it any further. Hours later while sitting in a dentist's chair, sheer terror struck me. I cannot tell you why because I had never experienced such a feeling before. Can you see where I am going with this? Second Timothy 1:7 came flooding back into my thoughts. I began quoting this verse with my mouth propped wide open at the dentist—and peace returned!

What you read will come back to you when needed. Nothing happens by accident, and that Scripture did not just pop into my head right when I woke up just for the fun of it. Remember, God is watching over His Word to perform it, and it will accomplish that for which He sent it. Trust this process. There have been many times when I have said, "I remember that Scripture, but I cannot tell you exactly where it is located." However, I can roughly quote it. Perfection of memorization of Scripture is not required, but the truth of what is being said is.

IMPLEMENT SCRIPTURE MEMORIZATION

The best way to begin addressing an emotion or fear or any negative thought is to open a concordance at the back of your Bible or obtain a regular complete concordance, and read as many scriptures as possible. For example, if you are bound by anger, find every Scripture on anger, and read them. If you are bound by fear, read every Scripture on peace. If you struggle with knowing your worth, then read Scriptures on the love of God. This is the place to start.

I do not usually recommend skipping around the Bible like that, but right now, you need to know and fix your thoughts on the promises of God. You can take time to read or study a specific book later. Right now, it is focus time!

Once you begin to find Scriptures that speak life to you, write some of them down on cue cards and place them all around you home, car, or office. I love visiting family because they have cue cards all around their bedrooms, bathrooms, and kitchens that are different than the ones I have posted in my home. Not into cue cards? Plaster Scripture on your iPad, computer, or phone screen. Hang pictures with your favorite verses. Wear clothing that declares the goodness of God. Purchase a wallet with a Scripture on it. Drink tea or coffee from mugs that recite your favorite verse. The point? Immerse yourself in the Word of God so that your mind is renewed, your thoughts zeroed in on Jesus, and you are operating in the mind of Christ.

Paul reminds us that we have the same mindset as Jesus (1 Corinthians 2:14-16; Philippians 2:5). What would this resemble on a daily basis? We would exhibit the fruit of the Spirit—love, joy, peace, patience, kindness, goodness, faithfulness, gentleness, and self-control (Galatians 5:22-23). It is fully possible to display this fruit even when events occur that shatter our world. How did Jesus respond when hell was breaking loose on Him? He prayed. He told God that He would be obedient because Jesus knew His Father was with Him.

SCRIPTURES

Here are a few scriptures I feel led to write, in addition to all the other Scriptures already mentioned in this chapter. There are so many more, but I want to help you begin the process of allowing the Word of God to bring life into your weary and possibly worn out soul.

"And my God will meet all your needs according to the riches of his glory in Christ Jesus" —Philippians 4:19

"But he was pierced for our transgressions, he was crushed for our iniquities; the punishment that brought us peace was upon him, and by his wounds we are healed" —Isaiah 53:5

"In all these things we are more than conquerors through him who loved us" —Romans 8:37

"I sought the Lord, and he answered me; he delivered me from all my fears. The angel of the Lord encamps around those who fear him, and he delivers them" —Psalm 34:4,7

"One who has unreliable friends soon comes to ruin, but there is a friend who sticks closer than a brother" —Proverbs 18:24

"If any of you lacks wisdom, you should ask God, who gives generously to all without finding fault, and it will be given to you" —James 1:5

"Peace I leave with you; my peace I give you. I do not give to you as the world gives. Do not let your hearts be troubled and do not be afraid" —James 1:5

"The Lord is good, a refuge in times of trouble. He cares for those who trust in him" —Nahum 1:7

"Whoever dwells in the shelter of the Most High will rest in the shadow of the Almighty. I will say of the Lord, 'He is my refuge and my fortress, my God in whom I trust'"   —Psalm 91:1-2

"Trust in the Lord with all your heart and lean not on your own understanding; in all your ways submit to him, and he will make your paths straight"   —Proverbs 3:5-6

"He must become greater; I must become less"   —John 3:30

"Keep your lives free from the love of money and be content with what you have, because God has said, 'Never will I leave you; never will I forsake you.' So we say with confidence, 'The Lord is my helper; I will not be afraid. What can mere mortal do to me?'"   —Hebrews 13:5-6

"Jesus Christ is the same yesterday and today and forever"
          —Hebrews 13:8

Allow God's Word to get down inside you, to the depths of your soul. Base decisions on these Scriptures. Compare every thought to the Word. How does it compare? If it does not line up to what God says, then tear that thought down, and bring it into the obedience of Christ (2 Corinthians 10:5). What do I mean by this? If a voice comes into your thinking that says nothing will ever change, then speak back to that thought, and say, "All things are possible with God" (Matthew 19:26) or "All things work together for the good of those who love the Lord and are called according to His purposes" (Romans 8:28).

His Word is powerful and alive! Do not allow negative thinking to dictate your life any longer. You cannot choose what thoughts come into your mind, but you can choose what you will think on. However, this is only part of the battle. What else can you do to overcome and live a victorious, transformed life? Wage war. Do not settle in the wilderness but fight for the Promised Land. Keep reading to learn how.

CHAPTER 6

WAGING WAR

*"I believe that the attacks on your life have much
more to do with who you might be in the future
than who you have been in the past."*
—Lisa Bevere

Lisa Bevere's statement above is so true. The enemy only fights against things of which he is afraid. A mighty plan must be on your life for the battle to be so intense, thus provoking a confrontation. This is the reason the war is waging and why this whole chapter focuses solely on fighting. "Doing battle" refers to overcoming, working through, and dealing with whatever has you entangled so you can walk victoriously through life. When we are spiritually, mentally, and emotionally healthy, we decrease the potential to feel overwhelmed, confused, discouraged, angry, or any other negative emotion.

One of the areas identified in this book's chapter entitled "Finding Peace with God" recognizes that He fights for us.

Scripture says God is our vindicator (Psalm 7:8). When we allow Him to step in front, we can rest assured that resolution will occur. James 4:7 says, "Submit yourselves then to God. Resist the devil, and he will flee." When we surrender the problem, attitude, or sin to the Lord and then wait on Him to act, He dominates whatever is buffeting us. The main contest is not ours, but we do play an important role on how long the assault lasts—we must resist giving up.

Second Corinthians 10:4 declares, "The weapons we fight with are not the weapons of the world. On the contrary, they have divine power to demolish strongholds." First, do you notice that we are given weapons? These weapons are God-given. There is no need on our part to mentally wrestle to figure out battle tactics or the enemy's weak points. Second, the power in the weapons is supernatural. Nothing in our own strength can defeat what attacks us in the spiritual realm. Last, these armaments are meant to destroy anything that keeps us from living in God's best.

Before I begin discussing the artillery, I want to say something about the quickness of divine intervention. If you read through the Bible, you will see "suddenly "or "but God." These words are important, identifying a rapid shift in course and representing that God has shown up. Do you need a "suddenly" or a "but God" right now?

JAMIE

Jamie was an alcoholic who was depressed and also suffered with agoraphobia, the fear of leaving one's home. One night, she became so desperate, she called out to the Lord in her bedroom without even really knowing Him. In that one moment of time, she was completely delivered of everything that held her bound—

alcohol, depression, and fear. She experienced a suddenly! Now Jamie is the lead pastor of a church, a revivalist, author, podcast host, and mighty intercessor. She remains a daily warrior for Jesus!

The battleground is one of the most prominent places for believers because this is where we spend most of our life, even without recognizing it. I believe there are some things that transpire in the spiritual realm we have no idea ensued. When we engage in warfare on a regular basis, the plans of the enemy are thwarted before they can ever come to fruition. If you are experiencing a battle right now, your "suddenly" may just come as you read this chapter.

So, how do we respond when the war is raging? I believe God clearly identifies methods for us to employ. Instead of trying to control it, change it, or overcome it on our own, we can trust that He has our back. What powerful weapons do we wield? They include but are not limited to the following: abiding in the Vine, putting on the armor of God, speaking the Word, thinking on the truth, praise and worship, loving others, increasing our faith, praying without ceasing, not wallowing in our trial, having joy, living by wisdom, guarding our heart, knowing that He is God, keeping our peace, and walking in grace.

ABIDE IN THE VINE

There is tremendous power and authority available to us when we abide in the Lord. Standing firm in Him remains impossible when we do not remain linked to Him as He instructs us to (John 15). Scripture says that when we abide in Christ (described as the "Vine" in John 15, with us as the "branches"), we will bear much fruit, but that apart from Him, we can do nothing (John

15:4). What does it mean to "remain" in Him? It means to stay connected to or draw strength from Him. We accomplish this by continued intimacy through prayer and communication. In 2020, quarantining had us sequestered in our homes to stay healthy. The confines of that space were our protection. That is what the Lord is talking about when He says, "remain in me."

God is the originator of our strength. He is not *one of many* power sources, but the source. When we cut ties with Him, the battle will overtake us. Are you connected to the Vine right now? Is His life-giving, divine, supernatural virtue flowing through you as you stand on the battleground? If yes, wonderful. If not, reach out your hand, and take the Lord's. He is waiting right now. What are you waiting for?

PUT ON THE ARMOR OF GOD

The second area to discuss in terms of the powerful weapons God provides for us is the armor of God, introduced in Ephesians 6:

> *Finally, be strong in the Lord and in his mighty power. Put on the full armor of God, so that you can take your stand against the devil's schemes. For our struggle is not against flesh and blood, but against the rulers, against the authorities, against the powers of this dark world and against the spiritual forces of evil in the heavenly realms. Therefore, put on the full armor of God, so that when the day of evil comes you may be able to stand your ground, and after you have done everything, to stand. Stand firm then, with a belt of truth buckled around your waist, with the breast plate of righteousness in place, and with your feet fitted with the readiness that comes from the gospel of peace. In addition to all this, take up the shield of faith, with which you can extinguish all the*

flaming arrows of the evil one. Take the helmet of salvation and the sword of the spirit, which is the word of God. —vv. 10-17

God supplies the protective coverings for our battles. This armor He willingly gives us empowers us to stand against the enemy. The key that operates the effectiveness of these pieces of armory is that *we* must *clothe ourselves* with them. A conscious choice activates the placement of each weapon. We must put on the full suit, as all parts are necessary to settle firmly in our place. We eventually become the victors!

What are these pieces of armor? The first piece mentioned is the belt of truth, and we are to tighten it. The belt of truth is the centerpiece of the armor. It goes around our waist, the part of our body that stabilizes and grounds us the most. We must know the truth of God's Word. This is the reason I encourage you to read the Word regularly. How can we tighten something when there is nothing to grab hold of, if we do not know what truth is?

The breastplate of righteousness follows, running from the top of the chest and usually covering all the way down past the pelvic area, to protect all the vital organs—heart, lungs, and so on. What is righteousness? It means being in a right relationship with the Lord through the blood of the Cross. When a person accepts Christ, the breastplate protects him or her from evil and deception.

Next, we must put on the gospel of peace. The important aspect of this piece of armor is to walk in the good news of Jesus. The gospel allows us to have a firm footing, just as the soldiers used to have nails on the bottom of their sandals so their feet would not slip. Because we know peace, we do not have to walk in fear.

The shield of faith covers almost the entire body. A shield in Roman times would have been similar in height to the soldier hoisting it. This cover prevents the fiery darts that the enemy slings at us from penetrating our being. The attacks are quickly stymied, and we are unharmed. Faith goes before us and is always out front of everything else.

The helmet of salvation is a heavy item that covers the entire head. The helmet is vital to protect the brain because if the head is injured, the warrior is of little use. Figuratively, when we place the helmet of salvation on, our identification of knowing who we are in Christ and who He is as our Savior, is protected. It keeps our thoughts in line with the Word of God and reassures us that no one can snatch us from His hand (John 10:28).

The last piece of armor is the sword, which is the Word of God. The sword is our only offensive weapon. More information about this will be presented in the next section.

The culmination of all these items is a complete suit of armor that nothing can penetrate. But do you notice how they only protect the front of us? We are not meant to run from the enemy but stand face-to-face as the Lord is our rear guard (Isaiah 52:12). When we engage in warfare fully suited up with God's protection, then no weapon formed against us shall prosper (Isaiah 54:17).

SPEAK THE WORD

I briefly touched upon this concept a couple of times in this book, but now I want to go into detail. In the previous chapter I revealed Scriptures that talk about how the Word is alive and powerful and will accomplish that for which the Lord sends it. But what about the Word makes it powerful and effective? Speaking it! If you say you are more than a conqueror, then you will be because that lines up with the Word of God. Speak the Word every day, even multiple times a day, to bring life, peace, clarity, strength, and joy into your situation.

Proverbs 18:21 tells us, "The tongue has the power of life and death, and those who love it will eat its fruit." What is that Scripture really saying to us? What we speak will bring either positive or negative outcomes. Genesis 1 repeatedly shows an important pattern: God said ... and then it was so. As God was creating, He accomplished His work with a spoken word. There is creative power in the words that go forth from your mouth.

What are you saying on the battleground? As you stand and wait on the Lord, are you releasing life over yourself, your family, ministry, career, or finances? What comments reach into the spiritual realm and pull down blessings? Repeat God's promises, such as: I can do all things through Christ who strengthens me, God will meet my needs, by the stripes on Jesus's back I am healed, God will never leave me nor forsake me, all my sins are all washed away by the cross. If you speak a curse or death by regurgitating the lies of the enemy such as: things will never change, this is too hard, I can't handle this anymore, I am unlovable, or I cannot break this addiction, then cease immediately!

In Romans 4, Paul addresses how Abraham's offspring are included in the promise originally given to him, which only comes by faith. Paul refers in verse 17 to "the God who gives life to the dead and calls into being things that were not." Your life may not reflect what you desire yet, but speak as if it does. For example, say "God is changing my circumstances. God has provided a way out. God is meeting my every need." Speak life!

The battleground is a serious place and for people to overcome life's hardships when unwilling to give up. What you speak reveals

TRANSFORMED

your level of trust in the Lord. In a previous chapter I wrote a few
of my favorite Scriptures, but right now I encourage you to write
down yours and begin speaking them daily. When you begin to
have negative thoughts, speak the Word of God against them.
You will notice how quickly strength returns and gives life.

THINK ON THESE THINGS

Like speaking the Word, this section directs us to contemplate
positive things. In the previous chapter I wrote about having
the mind of Christ. One way to accomplish this is to meditate
on things that are true, lovely, honorable, just, kind, winsome,
and gracious. Paul pleads with us to fix our mind on these things
(Philippians 4:8). While attending a Joyce Meyer conference, I
remember her proclaiming that where the mind goes, the person
follows. This is so true. What you allow yourself to think about
will become your reality. If you ponder on the faithfulness of
God, then you will trust Him more. If you speculate about how
horrible your life is, however, then your situation will worsen.

The main type of theory I utilize in counseling is called
cognitive therapy. This is when people identify negative and
distorted thought patterns then reframe those thoughts into a
healthier way of thinking. This is what Paul is encouraging the
people of Philippi to do: deliberate on things that bring life and
encouragement, instead of the lies of the enemy, the world, or
one's own self-talk.

One technique often utilized is called "thought stopping."
When a person begins to have negative thoughts, they are
instructed to tell themself to "stop" out loud and replace that
thought with the truth of God. One lady came into a session and
confessed she had to repeat this method what appeared to be a

thousand times because her thinking was so negative, but she did not give up. Employ this tactic as often as you need it, until it becomes a habit. This is where knowing the Word of God is vital. If you know what the promises of the Lord are, then you can think on those things. In addition, if you know what the Word of God says about who you are in Christ, then you can rest assured that you are good enough, loved enough, and thought of. So, what are your thoughts right now?

PRAISE AND WORSHIP

Psalm 100:4 reminds us, "Enter his gates with thanksgiving and his courts with praise; give thanks to him and praise his name." Another mighty weapon in our arsenal is praise and worship. We enter God's presence with thanksgiving. Remaining focused on what we are thankful for makes it much more difficult to become discouraged or weary. An attitude of gratitude is vital on the battleground.

The second aspect is that we enter His courts with praise. We approach God with thanksgiving and then are drawn even closer to Him through praise, which prompts us to remember how great and mighty our God is.

I remember a time of brokenness when I felt overwhelmed, and I heard that still small voice saying *praise Me*. Initially all I could muster was raised hands as tears flowed down my cheeks. I was unable to sing along with the praise music, but my heart was connecting with the words. Before I knew it, the tears dried up and the words rang forth from my mouth. The heaviness lifted, and joy replaced it. God alone can do that! With just ten minutes of praising and worshiping Him, my focus shifted from my problems to His sovereignty, His goodness, and His faithfulness.

This is the purpose of praise—to take the focus off ourselves and our situations to redirect our attention back on the Lord. When the presence of God permeates, the devil must flee.

Praise can happen anywhere, anytime, and without music. Praise comes from knowing who God really is. A helpful suggestion is to begin with the letter A in the alphabet and go all the way to Z with words that describe God. In your car, in the shower, or at work, the location is irrelevant. The only aspect that matters is follow through.

Worship is not only singing but also a lifestyle. We can worship God by what we do, how we act, and where we spend our resources. Amid sorrow, feelings of betrayal, or the need to control, we can choose to worship the Creator of the universe and live with integrity and honesty. We can continue to tithe even when finances are tight and the bottom line of our income and expenses does not add up. These actions reveal a heart set on the Lord, even if life appears to be unraveling or unstable.

LOVE OTHERS

One of the ways we worship God and do battle is to love others just as Jesus commands us to (John 13:34). Paul reminds us in Romans 12:21, "Do not be overcome by evil, but overcome evil with good." The quickest way to get the upper hand in combat is to love others. When the devil would rather you hide and stick your head in the sand, or even worse, lash out and say something mean or spiteful, this is when you do something good for someone else. Watch how quickly your attitude will change and the view of your situation alter when you begin to reach out to others.

In Ephesians 6:12, Paul clarifies that we wrestle not with flesh and blood. Recognition that people are not our problem assists in loving others. You may think that your spouse, child, or boss is to blame when in reality it is evil motivating them to act. It is not them personally with whom you battle. This is essential for you to know.

When my husband and I went through a season of trial, God informed me that Kraig was not the issue. Therefore, I refused to fight with him because I knew he was not the problem. I fought on my knees in prayer. Even when the church plant closed, I was not angry at the people in the city, but with the enemy for keeping them blinded.

The enemy wants you to become mad at people and latch onto resentment, bitterness, and anger in order to gain a foothold on your mind and heart to destroy relationships. However, when you acknowledge this fact, you can intercede on your knees and overcome with love. When you refuse to allow anger to continue, not only will you have peace with God, but you will have peace with other people. This is critical at this point on the battleground. Arguments are the last interaction you need. When you are struggling emotionally, you may find yourself being less tolerant of people. Remember, it is the enemy who wants to bind you, so take a deep breath and a step back.

INCREASE YOUR FAITH

Hebrews 11:6 explains, "And without faith it is impossible to please God, because anyone who comes to him must believe that he exists and that he rewards those who earnestly seek him." Many refer to Hebrews 11 as the "Great Hall of Faith," as it recounts the testimonies of some of the most successful people in the Bible. Why was it important for the author of Hebrews to recite these stories? Because we all need a faith boost!

We are unable to please God unless we walk in faith, as Hebrews 11:6 notes. We must believe that when we pray, He hears us; that when we are in need, He will take care of us; and that when we are sick, He will heal us. We continue to press into Him because there is an assurance that blessings will flow when we are connected to Him.

But how does a person increase their faith? Does the Bible not say that each of us has been given a measure of faith by God (Romans 12:3)? If what we have has already been given, how can we obtain more? Paul instructs us that faith comes through hearing the gospel through the Word (Romans 10:17). Again, studying Scripture is imperative. Not only does it bring life, freedom, and healing, but it actually increases our faith. Faith grows the most when we lean into the Lord in times of desperation.

Another avenue to boost our confidence is to hear other people's God stories. Ask friends and family members to share with you what the Lord has done in their lives. Watch verified YouTube videos, listen to podcast interviews, or read books on revivals; there are a myriad of possibilities to grasp the faithfulness of the Lord. We overcome by the blood of the Lamb and the word of our own testimony (Revelation 12:11). When you recognize that if God did a miracle for someone else, it is also possible in your life. This increases expectations for Him to present Himself mighty in your life.

PRAY WITHOUT CEASING

Paul mentions in Ephesians 6:18 to pray at all times, and without ceasing. This is a warrior attitude. Psalm 50:15 states, "Call on me in the day in trouble; I will deliver you, and you will honor me." God wants you to pray about everything. Do not think anything is too small or trivial because everything about you is important to Him.

Some people discontinue prayer when wracked with guilt. Do not cease calling on the Father. On the other hand, ask God to help you defeat the sins you struggle with. Do not become embarrassed or shameful but ask for strength to quit doing what you know you should not be doing.

Another reason people stop crying out to the Lord is unanswered prayer. I encourage you to press on and persevere in prayer. I believe that as a body of believers we have lost the desire and ability to travail. By "travail" I mean the need to press in until we feel a release in our spirit that what we have asked for is resolved. One morning, all the sudden I felt an intense drawing to pray for my father. Every time I attempted to stand up and move on with my day, I was brought back to my knees. I am unsure how long this lasted, but finally I was released. I learned a couple of days later that my father had passed out in his garden and had lain in the field. After a short time, he stood up and went inside the home. When I pressed for more details—yes, you guessed it— that was the exact time I travailed for him. I remain amazed at how the Lord moves us to impact the lives of others. You never know what someone is encountering when you are led by the Spirit to pray.

On multiple occasions Jesus instructed His disciples to pray in His name to the Father, saying it would be granted. Now, I will be the first to admit not understanding why sometimes we intercede for someone to be healed and they are not healed (in the earthy realm). I do not claim to have the answer to those questions, but what I do know is the persistent widow parable where Jesus instructs us to continue to cry out for help (Luke 18:1-8). Do not give up! God hears your prayers and will answer. We must stand firm on the belief that He is a rewarder of those who cry out to Him.

DO NOT WALLOW IN YOUR PAIN

First Corinthians 10:13 states, "No temptation has overtaken you except what is common to mankind. And God is faithful; he will not let you be tempted beyond what you can bear. But when you are tempted, he will also provide a way out so that you can endure it." Many people focus on the section of this Scripture that details how God does not give us more than we can handle. I believe this is true, unless for a deeper reason. Sometimes we go through events that we cannot get through on our own, but the Lord always provides us the way out of it—Himself! Calling out and leaning into God are the ways we endure and embrace victory.

However, I want to take it further. When we encounter trials, the devil endeavors to decrease our focus with lies to distract us from Jesus. When this transpires, we remove our eyes from the Lord and place them squarely on what stares us straight in the face. This is exactly what Peter did; he began to sink when he took his eyes off Jesus and looked at the waves around him (Matthew 14:22-33). The point? The Lord is the way out, but we must remain laser focused on Him.

What you currently face may feel overwhelming and difficult, yet the problem did not originate in your life. That is one aspect of the Scripture I find comforting and yet disturbing. No temptation has overtaken you except what is common to every person. Unfortunately, the enemy wants to destroy our lives. Our mindset at times tricks us into believing that no one can comprehend or understand what we are experiencing or feeling. That is a lie from Satan and is meant to keep you bound.

First Peter 5:8-9 emphasizes this same point, "Be alert and of sober mind. Your enemy the devil prowls around like a roaring lion looking for someone to devour. Resist him, standing firm in the faith, because you know that the family of believers throughout the world is undergoing the same kind of sufferings." You are not alone, but you must keep your thoughts centered on Jesus. Nothing you are experiencing is new; there are people who understand.

From a counseling perspective, I encourage people to take an honest evaluation if they feel stuck in a victim mindset—a belief that everyone is out to get them, which triggers a detrimental philosophy. This state of mind attributes actions from others toward them as harmful and unfair, and views their circumstances as hopeless and unchangeable. They feel betrayed when others do not appear to care or see events according to their interpretation. Heightened feelings of anger, frustration, and depression result. This transpires even when there is proof of the opposite in their life. Everyone is not out to get you.

James 1:2-4 encourages us, "Consider it pure joy, my brothers and sisters, whenever you face trials of many kinds, because you know that the testing of your faith produces perseverance. Let perseverance finish its work so that you may be mature and complete, not lacking anything." When going through difficult times, there is always a choice—draw near to God or walk away. These verses remind us that difficult events are painful yet can be fruitful if we allow them to sift us and remove ungodly aspects of our personality. Why? Because the Lord wants us to lack nothing. He wants us to be complete in Him.

Cease wallowing in your trial and permit unhealthy thoughts in your heart and attitude to be cut off. The longer you complain, the longer you will remain there. Realize there is only one way out of your situation—God's way. We cannot rush the process or sidestep the obstacle, no matter how hard we try. Trust me, I have tried. I also have learned that the more I push against my circumstances by taking over in my own strength and ability to fix them, the more negative my mindset becomes from frustration and exhaustion. The same is true, no doubt, with you. Sometimes we need to hear that we just need to get a better attitude and move beyond our self. People who grovel in their trials tend to be self-centered and desire sympathy or attention. If you have felt convicted in this area, ask God to help you cease this mentality. To balance this, sometimes crying is healthy, and talking with others is necessary.

HAVE JOY

There was tremendous pressure from outsiders to get the Israelites to cease building the wall around Jerusalem during Nehemiah's time. To encourage the people, Ezra reminded the people that it was the joy of the Lord that strengthened them (Nehemiah 8:10). Joy is not based on our circumstances but on our view. Is your focus on your problems or on God's greatness? You can have joy during suffering if your eyes are on Jesus instead of on what is encroaching.

One of the most effective methods to remain joyful—full of joy—is to praise God and read His Word. Wake up every morning and make the decision to have joy. Declare that this is the day the Lord has made; rejoice and be glad in it (Psalm 118:24), or you can wake up and say, "Not another day!" The choice is yours. If your joy decreases throughout the day—I know mine tends to do this—then reorient your thoughts.

Paul also reminds us to always rejoice in the Lord (Philippians 4:4). Rejoice means to realign our thoughts to joy. Paul was writing Philippians during a time of imprisonment, and chances are he was standing in waste, since prisons were underground. If he could declare joy in the midst of that circumstance, then we can also.

LIVE BY WISDOM

Walking in wisdom is essential when we are hurting. We tend to react based on emotions and not with a mind of Christ. As a counselor, I encourage people to focus on what they know, not on how they feel. Yes, it is important to recognize our feelings—but detrimental to be controlled by them. Proverbs 4:5-6 states, "Get wisdom, get understanding; do not forget my words or turn away from them. Do not forsake wisdom, and she will protect you; love her and she will watch over you." When we walk in wisdom, there is protection from the Lord. When we walk according to how we feel, then regrets, guilt, and more problems transpire.

The best way to walk in wisdom is to take time when making decisions or responding to conflict. Take a day or two to pray about them. When having to deal with a difficult situation immediately, do not just speak the first thing that comes to mind, but quietly pray and ask the Spirit to give you the needed words. You must make a conscious choice to walk according to wisdom and not how you feel in the moment. You cannot always trust your emotions. You may feel afraid, but you do not have to respond in fear. You may feel all alone, but you are not because God is with you.

How does a person gain more wisdom? James 1:5 tells us, "If any of you lacks wisdom, you should ask God, who gives generously to all without finding fault, and it will be given to you." Do you need more wisdom? Ask the Lord, and He will give it to you. Wisdom is not having everything figured out but inviting Christ into your thinking to see things the way He does. It is having the perspective of God on a situation since He is not hindered by earth's timeframe or resources. Wisdom is responding with the mind of Christ (Philippians 2:5-8). God will not judge you because you ask for insight. He desires to give it. He wants you to walk in His ways. Begin today to ask the Lord to give you this divine wisdom.

GUARD YOUR HEART

Whatever is in the heart rises to the surface. If you have anger in your heart, you will respond in anger. If you have jealousy in your heart, you will act out for attention. If you have resentment in your heart, selfishness will result. From the heart springs our behaviors. You cannot hide what is in your heart because it affects what you think and how you act. God sees and knows all, and by the way, most people can as well.

The Bible instructs, "Above all else, guard your heart, for everything you do flows from it" (Proverbs 4:23). Ask the Lord to help you guard your heart. It is during times of difficulty or trials that different roots can gain a foothold, such as resentment, anger, discouragement, or depression. If unprotected, further consequences result, which only complicates matters even more. You do not need this.

Along these same lines, ask the Lord to search your heart and identify any attitudes and beliefs that need to be challenged and dispelled. Jeremiah reminds us how deceitful the heart is (Jeremiah 17:9). Who alone can know it? Only the Lord truly knows what prompted David to cry out to Him in desperation, "Search me, Lord" (Psalm 139:23-24). When deceitful thoughts are detected, then exchange them with holy thinking.

KNOW THAT HE IS GOD

In a previous chapter, I addressed the need to be still and know that God is God. When the war is raging, it is vital to sit still in His presence. There is nothing like basking in the sun, sitting in a tree stand, or sipping a cup of coffee while the Lord reminds you who He is.

During times of pain, people attempt to distract themselves by always moving around or staying busy to prevent reflection on the pain and uncomfortable feelings that buffet them. I am not saying this is wrong—trust me, I do this—but we have to make sure that time is set aside to meditate on God and invite Him into our current situation. A friend of mine once asked me, "Kristi, does God need to Velcro you to that chair again?" If you do not take time to be still, God will give you opportunities to do this. Trust me, it is a lesson you do not want to learn the hard way. As I reflect, those times of being still in my life became treasured moments. I continue this practice daily. When we sense His presence, it brings such reassurance that this too shall pass.

KEEP YOUR PEACE

In John 14:27, Jesus informed His disciples that He had given them peace—not the world's fleeting calmness, but everlasting assurance. He has granted us this same peace. I love how the

Amplified Bible continues, instructing believers, "Let My perfect peace calm you in every circumstance and give you courage and strength for every challenge." We have a choice—to let or allow. We can continue to permit things to bother us, or we can rest assured that He is with us and fighting for us.

David reminds us in Psalm 34:14, "Turn from evil and do good; seek peace and pursue it." Again, this is a reminder of choice on our part. Peace just does not come on its own. One way to implement this option is to do good. Peace is next to impossible when actions and attitudes are contrary to the instruction of the Lord. To "pursue" means to go after—not a passive behavior but one of movement. Your pastor cannot give you peace. Your mother cannot give you peace. You alone must pursue it and go after it.

What is stifling your peace right now? Ask God to reveal what stole it. When He unveils it, make a choice to release it to Him. I pray right now that the Spirit of peace would engulf you, that you would sense Him coming upon you right now in the name of Jesus. May the worries and concerns of the world fall off your shoulders, and may you release fear right now in the name of Jesus. Amen! Do you sense His peace?

LIVE IN GRACE

God is loving and forgiving. His grace carries us through each day. Paul was experiencing a problem, only one of many, I might add. The Bible does not share exactly what it was but does detail the conversation between him and the Lord. Paul prayed for the thorn in his flesh to be removed. Did God take it away? No. But here was God's response in 2 Corinthians 12:9, "My grace is sufficient for you, for my power is made perfect in weakness."

Paul responds to the Lord's reply in the rest of that verse and the next by declaring, "Therefore I will boast all the more gladly about my weaknesses, so that Christ's power may rest on me. That is why, for Christ's sake, I delight in weaknesses, in insults, in hardships, in persecutions, in difficulties. For when I am weak, then I am strong."

What an awesome reminder. God is at His strongest in our lives when we are at our weakest. This is shouting time for somebody! God can come into your life the strongest when you feel all hell breaking lose. Satan thought you were an easy target, but he was deceived. The army of heaven stands in front of you, around you, and behind you. This reminds me of the Scripture where Elisha asks the Lord to open the eyes of his servant because fear had gripped his heart when he saw the enemy's army had surrounded the city. God answered Elisha's prayer, and the servant saw in the spiritual realm the hills full of horses and chariots of fire all around him and Elisha (2 Kings 6:17). What a beautiful picture of our Father.

The battle continues all around you, but you must continue to wage war. The battle is the Lord's, but you are on the battle-ground. You cannot escape it, but you can defeat it! Do all you can and let the Lord do the rest. Stand fast and see the deliverance of the Lord!!

CHAPTER 7

FORGIVENESS

*"To forgive is to set a prisoner free
and discover that the prisoner was you."*
—Lewis B. Smedes

I hope thus far in the book you have sensed the Holy Spirit
ministering to you and that a strength and resolve have been
building, and that today is a better day than yesterday. Your
future is brightening, and the awareness of the potential God has
placed within you is rising.

ROY

Roy did not grow up in a family unit even though he had both
parents and siblings. Both parents were alcoholics while he was
a child, and he has no memories of his parents being married.
His mother was married over five different times. His childhood
could be described as dysfunctional with little mental or emotional

security. His mother would leave him with family members for long periods of time, which brought about abandonment, fear, and relationship issues. Roy spent a significant amount of time living with his aunt and uncle from the age of ten to fifteen. They were devout Christian believers, which brough stability to his life. He even went into the military for a period.

Roy spent time in the Word of God for the Lord to transform his thinking and renew his mind, because he quickly learned he could not change himself. Anger and resentment toward his mother lingered into adulthood, and he kept his own children from her. It was not one prayer or one moment that resulted in forgiving his mother but everyday spiritual disciplines. Roy believes his life is nothing short of a miraculous transformation from shame, fears, insecurities, and abandonment issues. Feelings of insignificance were erased by the revelation that he is dearly loved and created by God. He took hold of Jeremiah 29:11 that the Lord had a plan for his life. Roy has now been a senior pastor for over twenty years, completing his Doctor of Ministry degree, and he serves as Executive Presbyter for the south region of the Illinois District of the Assemblies of God. God is using him in powerful ways and only because he latched onto the Lord and built his foundation on biblical truth. The relationship with his mother is healed and she attends the same church he pastors.

Just like Roy, you are now at a fork in the road. You will either embark on a journey that continues to produce freedom or on a journey that will greatly hinder your forward progress. As you look to the right way or to a diverted path, you choose the direction. You can tell by this chapter's title what the subject is— forgiveness. Perhaps no one comes to mind at this moment who you feel you need to forgive but do keep reading. As you read through the chapter, ask God to reveal to you if this is an issue in your heart. Be open. Be honest.

THE IMPORTANCE OF FORGIVENESS

Forgiveness is essential in life. No one exists without facing this dilemma. Remember, we are all fallen individuals who live in a disastrous world. Sin entered through a choice Adam and Eve made in the Garden of Eden, which created a chasm between humans and God (Genesis 3). When God created us, He gave us freewill. Sometimes we make decisions that are detrimental to others and to ourselves. Therefore, sin enters, and the need for forgiveness becomes a reality.

Throughout the years, I have heard many reasons (and excuses) why people do not forgive. The excuse that forgiveness is a personal issue that does not need to be discussed with anyone else has dominated the voices in my counseling office. I disagree. We are not an island unto ourselves. The routes we take impact everyone around us. I also often hear, "What happens if you are not quite sure *how* to forgive?" This is legitimate reasoning to a certain extent. The Bible provides many verses that instruct us how to forgive (a few will be addressed soon).

What if you are unsure if you need to forgive? Ask the Lord to search your heart. What happens if you think you have forgiven, but the same negative feelings continue to surface over and over? Does that mean you have not forgiven? These are all great questions and the reason for this chapter.

Every person is required to deal with forgiveness; we have established that. Whether one needs to forgive others only or also oneself, these questions are the main reason people enter my counseling room. From this we can decipher two main points: First, the refusal or inability to forgive leads to bondage and complicates life more than it needs to. Second, no one is perfect—except Jesus of course. Everyone makes mistakes, and sin is inevitable.

Before forgiveness is defined, let's identify how unforgiveness leads to bondage and affects us emotionally, mentally, behaviorally, physically, and spiritually. Our feelings, thoughts, and behaviors all interrelate. One cannot occur without affecting the others. These things also impact our physical and spiritual health, too.

Let us first look at emotions, interchangeable with the term *feelings*. When people react strictly on how they feel, the roller coaster has begun. The highs and lows are exhausting and frustrating. Yet, it is difficult to stop the cart on the track. What feelings come to your mind? Frequent emotions experienced when one feels hurt include anger, sadness, depression, irritability, anxiety, and shame. These feelings may serve as an underlying current on a day-to-day basis, or they may surface when the person who harmed you comes to mind or interacts with you.

Do you know that you can *choose* how you feel? You control what emotions you react to. You may feel unable to stop certain ones from rising within you, but you do not have to entertain them. You choose to be angry, bitter, or resentful. Yes, people may do things that harm you, but you are the one who ultimately chooses how you feel.

Wasn't Jesus justified to feel angry and bitter when He was rejected by the ones He came to save? Yes, He had every right. But He did not choose to feel that way because it would have hindered His purpose, just as anger and bitterness handicap our purposes when we allow such emotions to control us. Ouch! That hurt.

If your child was killed in a car accident by a drunk driver, are you justified to feel anger? Everyone would be angry, including myself. You may be justified to feel this way, but how long do you continue to feel negative? How long does the other person deserve to be punished? How long are you going to remain in bondage because of what someone else has done? (This reference is not towards the legal system here, which has its own laws and regulations that are not determined by us. People still have to justifiably face earthly consequences for any actions if the situation warrants.)

The grip of negative emotions can eat away at us on the inside. In most cases, as we hang onto the painful situation, the other person most likely has moved on and may not even know they hurt us. And if they do know, they may have already forgiven themselves or just do not care. This anger allows the situation to continue to impact one's view on life. I am not saying that if something horrific has happened in your life you should immediately no longer feel any negative feelings. That would be almost impossible. But the longer you hold onto negative emotions, the longer it takes you to release them.

If you think your emotions are not hindering you, think again. You may not display the emotion, but it surfaces in many other ways. The way you think, the way you act, the nature of your medical issues, and your spirituality are all impacted. And if you attempt to push down the negative feelings you experience, then one day you will explode. This leads to the next area that is impacted.

Negative thinking also coincides with the *refusal* to forgive. These thoughts may include trust issues, always looking for the worst in people, becoming critical of people, and so on. These negative thoughts can debilitate us. We hinder ourselves from seeing anything positive in the person we refuse to forgive and quite possibly in other people as well. Unfortunately, this impacts how we see God, as we at times project our feelings onto Him.

Additionally, negative thinking *triggers emotions* like depression and anxiety. The base of anxiety is fear. One way people compensate is to obsess over a situation to figure things out to decrease the uncomfortableness. Obsessive thinking gets triggered, and the event replays over and over in one's mind. Have you been going through the whole situation word for word? Obsessive thinking can turn into compulsive behavior, and a whole new set of issues arises, which leads us to the next topic.

Unhealthy actions result when we do not forgive. What we think impacts how we feel, which in turn dictates how we react. Unless we control and discard negative thoughts, they will turn into behaviors. Have you ever stopped going to a certain restaurant or even a church because the person who hurt you goes there? Let us go even deeper than just a change of location. One's conduct can originate or worsen to deal with pain by numbing oneself or trying to escape when unforgiveness rages. A few of these responses are getting even, drinking alcohol or using drugs to cover pain, gambling, overeating, or worse—suicide attempts.

Many people who turned to maladaptive behaviors to deal with the pain of unforgiveness in their life tend to enter counseling. If you are reading this book right now and recognize your own actions, cease these behaviors immediately. You are only hurting yourself when you respond this way. When you hold onto all the negative feelings, you invite the person to "live rent-free in your head." What does that mean? When you allow someone else to continue to affect how you feel long after the situation is over, your life revolves around the pain. The other person is brought into your today and your tomorrow. So, not only have they stolen something in your past, but now your future as well.

People who refuse to forgive tend to be bitter. Their actions toward others tend to be harmful. You know the saying, "hurting people hurt people." Whether it is having a sharp response to a question, ignoring someone, cutting people off in traffic, or other adverse reactions, these are all examples of thoughts and emotions coming out in behaviors. These actions simply continue the cycle of harm. Then *you* may end up needing to ask for forgiveness.

What happens when we hold onto anger in our thoughts, emotions, and behaviors? That anger *will* begin to impact us physically, with symptoms such as heart problems, stomach problems, high blood pressure, high cholesterol, breathing problems, tiredness, and headaches. Do you have any of these symptoms right now? Is holding onto unforgiveness causing your health to deteriorate?

Last, anger hinders your relationship with the Lord. For the most part, people pull away from the Lord or blame God for what happened to them. Therefore, their spiritual journey is abruptly halted or even abandoned.

You may be thinking right now, "But Kristi, I am still pressing into God, and my spiritual walk is not hindered because I have not forgiven the person." I respectfully disagree. Let me back up my stance with Scripture. In Matthew 6:12, Jesus is teaching the disciples the Lord's Prayer: "And forgive us our debts, as we also have forgiven our debtors." Here Jesus reminds the disciples to ask the Lord for forgiveness based on actions they have already accomplished. *Have forgiven* is past tense. When they pray to the Father and ask for forgiveness, they remind the Lord that they have *already* forgiven others. They provoke God to treat them the way they have treated others.

Jesus goes on in Matthew 6:14-15, telling His disciples, "For if you forgive other people when they sin against you, your heavenly father will also forgive you. But if you do not forgive others for their sins, your father will not forgive your sins." The bottom line? If you do not forgive others, then God will not forgive you. Your unforgiveness creates a broken relationship with Him. Your prayers go unheard. Your true peace is gone. This is the reason people turn to the world for peace.

Along the lines of your relationship being hindered with the Lord if you retain unforgiveness, 1 John 2:9-11 states, "Anyone who claims to be in the light but hates a brother or sister is still in the darkness. Anyone who loves their brother and sister lives in the light, and there is nothing in them to make them stumble. But anyone who hates a brother or sister is in the darkness and walks around in the darkness. They do not know where they are going, because the darkness has blinded them."

If you are holding onto unforgiveness, hear the heart of the Father right now. You are deceived by your anger and unforgiveness. Your rage has blinded you from the truth that your walk with the Lord has been and continues to be hindered. It is your choice to remain in bondage.

FORGIVENESS BEGINS WITH A CHOICE

Now that we have examined the impact of unforgiveness on us emotionally, mentally, physically, and spiritually, it is necessary to recognize that forgiveness begins with a *choice*. You may not *feel* ready to forgive. You may have an attitude that "I deserve to be angry." If you have been hurt on purpose, then those feelings are real and normal. If your husband hits you or you have been raped, then your feelings are justifiable. Again, these feelings are not wrong or abnormal. The question becomes, is it healthy to continue to hold onto them? There comes a certain point that you must decide if you want to remain in the pit of unforgiveness or move forward into healing.

You may be thinking right now that there really is nothing you are holding onto concerning unforgiveness. If this is true, great! However, I want to insert here that the best way to avoid having to address unforgiveness is to *quickly forgive*. Do not allow the pain of hurt to get a foothold in the beginning. Decide today to be a person not easily offended. When harm does come, quickly apply the blood of Jesus to the situation, turn it over to Him, and lean into Him for healing and vindication.

Perhaps nothing in your life requires forgiveness at present; no one has drastically harmed you, and life is good. If this is your experience, be grateful. However, can I challenge you on an everyday occurrence? Recently, in order to obtain my annual dental cleaning, I had to search for another dentist since my current one no longer accepted my insurance. I contacted a former dentist's office and asked if they took my insurance. The lady on the other end of the phone stated they could bill my insurance company. She scheduled an appointment which I attended. My teeth were cleaned, and x-rays obtained. In the process, a cavity was identified so a week later I returned to take care of that. However, the lady at the office did not clarify the complete truth. What turned into an assumption on my part that insurance would cover it based on the assistant's statement turned into an exceptionally large dental bill. Of course, I questioned the lady, but I became so angry. I excused myself from the phone call and had to process it with the Lord.

Why do I share this? Because daily opportunities in life exist where we must forgive. I refused to return to that office, but I had to forgive the lady. Do I feel like she was dishonest? Yes, to a certain extent. However, her business practices are irrelevant to my walk with God. If I want to remain connected to Him, I must forgive—period! I chose to release my anger to avoid getting stuck. You too must make choices every day that will keep the communication line to God open and clear or stop it up with the grime and gunk of the world.

This chapter is not intended to minimize what you have experienced or invalidate your pain but rather should serve to challenge your stance of unforgiveness. You may see the word *forgiveness* and think, "Surely, you cannot ask me to forgive?" Yes, I am. I encourage you to go to the place of tremendous pain and give it to the Lord. My only request is that you read the rest of the chapter before you ignore me. Let the truth of this chapter permeate your heart.

The Bible contains many verses on forgiveness, most likely because it is so difficult to forgive and because we can only do so through a divine act of the grace of God. Difficulty in forgiving stems from our carnal, human nature. We want the person or people that hurt us to have to pay or at least admit they are wrong and apologize.

Do you agree that all have sinned and fallen short of the glory of God (Romans 3:23)? Do you agree that you have not been perfect? Okay. This is a good starting point. We agree so far. No one is perfect, and we all make mistakes. Furthermore, if we are honest, we know we have intentionally said things or done things to hurt somebody's feelings, especially when it comes to a spouse, friend, or family member. We know how to push people's buttons.

Sin is sin and separates us all from our loving Father. One sin is not worse than another. Lying is a sin. Gossip is a sin. Stealing is a sin. And yes, hating someone is a sin. I think you get my point. If you have been holding onto unforgiveness and you have felt convicted already in this chapter, I encourage you to repent right now and ask the Lord to help you.

The first step to forgiveness is to ask the Lord to help you want to forgive. Trust me, God will answer that prayer. Sometimes it is easier to forgive someone if they have asked for forgiveness or they did not intentionally mean to hurt you. However, we are called to forgive even if someone's actions were reckless and willful.

You may be thinking, "But, Kristi, how many times do I need to forgive that person when they repeatedly do the same behavior over and over?" Jesus has the answer in Matthew 18:21-22, which says, "Then Peter came to Jesus and asked, Lord, how many times shall I forgive my brother or sister who sins against me? Up to seven times? Jesus answered, I tell you, not seven times, but seventy-seven times." The footnote in the NIV says or seventy times seven. That is a remarkable number of times to forgive someone. Jesus mentioned this because He knew the question would come up in our minds. How many times do I have to forgive my spouse, boss, parent, or child? The Lord's response was—as many times as they sin.

You and I are forgiven countless times in our lives and will never surpass the number required to forgive others. We sin daily;

remember—*all* sin separates us from God. God not only wants us to forgive so as not to hinder our relationship with Him but also so the devil cannot gain a foothold in our live. Unforgiveness opens the door for the devil to enter our life.

Paul reminds us in Ephesians 4:26-27, "'In your anger do not sin': Do not let the sun go down while you are still angry, and do not give the devil a foothold." When you and I remain angry and do not forgive, the devil has an open door to wreak havoc upon us. Life is difficult enough without offering the enemy an opportunity to make us miserable.

Hebrews 12:14-15 states, "Make every effort to live in peace with everyone and to be holy; without holiness no one will see the Lord. See to it that no one falls short of the grace of God and that no bitter root grows up to cause trouble and defile many." The Lord instructs us to live at peace with everyone—not for them alone, but for us also. If you have resentment in your heart, you are going to have trouble in relationships, even the ones you desire to have.

Bitterness creates a negative view of God, self, and others. Hurting people hurt people. It is time for the cycle of pain to stop. Let it cease with you.

When Jesus hung on the Cross and His clothes were divided up, instead of anger and bitterness, He asked God to forgive those hurting Him because, He said, they did not know what they were doing (Luke 23:24). Jesus knew the people who mocked and tortured Him had no idea who He really was. You and I could argue they knew exactly what they were doing. They knew they were killing a man named Jesus. Yes, but they had no idea of the ramifications of those behaviors. It resembles the above phrase that hurting people hurt people. They may know their behaviors are wrong, but they have no idea of the depth of pain their actions prompt.

FORGIVENESS DEFINED

Forgiveness is a process and can only be administered with the help of God. What does it mean to forgive? Forgiveness has a two-pronged definition. First, forgiveness entails letting go of the pain and hurt that resulted from the situation. And second, forgiveness entails no longer wanting to punish the person or people. So many people have professed forgiveness because they have moved beyond their pain, only to realize that they still want to punish the person.

Forgiveness is *not* defined as telling the other person what they did was okay. Forgiveness has nothing to do with accepting what someone has done to you, but to acknowledge that the situation occurred. There is a difference between acknowledging what someone has done to you and accepting it. Accepting means to receive it willingly or to submit to it. To acknowledge the action means to admit something happened relative to a certain fact or situation. That is a crucial point. Believing that you must accept what happened causes a lot of people to not forgive. If you believe that, be prepared to see forgiveness in a different light where freedom from bondage can occur.

Forgiveness is a personal gift. We need the release from the negative ramifications. We do not forgive just to ease someone else's guilt. We do not forgive others for them, but for us. How a person defines forgiveness is the cornerstone of whether the person will want to forgive.

STEPS TOWARD FORGIVENESS

First, we must willingly let go of the pain associated with the act of harm. In this moment, ask God to search your heart to reveal what remains hidden. Is there anger, resentment, bitterness, or any other negative emotion? Ask God to reveal negative thoughts or attitudes toward anyone. Be honest. If the Lord does bring light regarding a situation or person, openly acknowledge the pain to yourself. Identify how holding onto the negative situation has impacted your life—emotionally, mentally, physically, and in your walk with the Lord.

Once you become aware of what emotions you were experiencing, lay them at the cross. This is the second step in finding freedom through forgiving others. Once you have made the choice, ask the Lord to help you relinquish those negative aspects that you have been carrying. If you are like me, I have bargained with God in this area. "Lord, if they apologize, then I will forgive them. Lord, I will forgive them *after* I give them a piece of my mind!" Does this sound familiar? Jesus did not let me get away with it either.

Next, Scripture encourages us to love our enemies and pray for them. Begin doing this. Pray for the person or people who harmed you. The prayer does not need to be elaborate or long. It might be as simple as, "Lord, may they know Your presence today." This is not a "Lord, punish them for what they did" kind of prayer, but a request to bless them. Remember the dentist's office I mentioned above? Yes, I had to pray for the lady and that office to relinquish all anger, but you know what? It worked.

Continue to implement these three steps until you feel a release. If you still struggle with this, examine your life to reflect on how unforgiveness has really impacted you. Be honest. Then, evaluate how different life could be if you were no longer bound. If you need further assistance, reach out for help. Contact your pastor, a Christian counselor, friend, or family member to pray with you. If you experienced something traumatic, please seek professional help. Post-traumatic stress disorder is real, especially if your life was threatened.

CONTINUED FORGIVENESS

What happens when you thought you have forgiven and yet negative emotions and thoughts surface? Sometimes, forgiveness comes in stages. However, there might be multiple areas that need to be forgiven in one situation. You may need to forgive a person for not calling you. But because they did not call you, you might need to forgive them for what they did next. In addition, there are levels of pain. Harsh words may have been forgiven, yet the act of betrayal still lingers.

We have all done things in our lives of which we are not proud—perhaps even some things of which we are downright ashamed. Would you want someone to hold against you the things you were truly sorry for? Peter best states the principle of forgiveness: "Above all, love each other deeply, because love covers a multitude of sins" (1 Peter 4:8). God has called us to love others. You may not love the person who hurt you now, but show that person God's love by forgiving them.

This chapter is not intended to serve as an all-inclusive treatise on forgiveness but rather a first step to let you know the importance of forgiving and being healed. Again, forgiveness is a divine act. That is the reason so many scriptures in the Bible address the need to forgive. Pray and ask God to help you on this journey.

HOW DO WE FORGET?

One hindrance to forgiveness relates to the problem, "How do we forgive when we cannot forget?" God did not create us to have amnesia. We can reflect on what has happened in our past that we were able to move forward from. If we have accepted the grace of Jesus and moved forward, then we must recognize that His blood covers the sins of others also. We do not forget what we have done in the past, but we have allowed it to shape and mold us into who we have become. The same holds true with a person who has harmed you (or people who have harmed you). The same blood that covers you covers them. It is a matter of bringing the person to the foot of the cross. If God's grace covers our sin, then it covers theirs also. If we think about that person and have negative emotions, we have not fully forgiven. And when that happens, I encourage you to once again lay the person at the foot of the cross and say, "Lord, I choose to forgive again." Continue this until forgiveness is complete. It is possible!

I was recently talking with my husband about my past and sharing some of the difficult things that happened to me during my parents' divorce. He responded with sympathy for me. I reassured him that it was okay because there was no longer any pain associated with it. There was no negative response within me. I have to say at that moment, I was so excited! I know that is a weird word to use, but in that moment, I realized God had *completed* the forgiveness needed in my heart, and healing had resulted. I cannot tell you when that happened, only that it had.

The best response for us is to remain in the Lord's presence, allow Him to heal the wounds, and remove anything that hinders us from an intimate relationship with Him. For some of you that hindrance is unforgiveness in your heart. It is time to lay it down.

Time is short. Jesus is coming back, and God has a plan for your life. He purposes to use you in a mighty way to bring glory to His name. Do not allow what someone else did to keep you bound. It is time to release the person who has harmed you so you can step into your destiny.

Someone reading this right now has the Holy Spirit all over you, and the Lord is asking you a question right now. Will you say yes to Jesus by releasing unforgiveness? Remember the choice is yours. You cannot move forward without forgiveness. Do not be deceived by thinking unforgiveness is not impacting you. You are blinded by the scales of anger, resentment, and bitterness if you think it is not. Move forward now.

We know the story of Job and his severe trial. Yet at the end of it, the Lord instructed him to forgive his friends who had a judgmental and poor attitude toward him during his difficult time. Job 42:10 states, "After Job had prayed for his friends [for forgiveness], the Lord restored his fortunes and gave him twice as much as he had before." When you forgive, God restores what was lost and will bless you with more.

If you have made the choice to forgive and are submitting it unto the Lord, may the words of Joel 2:25-26 encourage you: "I will repay you for the years the locusts have eaten—the great locust and the young locust, the other locusts in the locust swarm—my great army that I sent among you. You will have plenty to eat, until you are full, and you will praise the name of the Lord, who has worked wonders for you; never again will my people be shamed." I pray that God redeems what was lost and that all shame leaves in the name of Jesus!

CHAPTER 8

HEALING THE CHILD WITHIN

"Until we reclaim our lost child, we have no inner sense of self, and gradually The Poser becomes who we really think we are."[11]
— Brennon Manning

Without getting too psychological, it is imperative to address what the inner child is. The "inner child" is the part within our core that is effortlessly delighted, playful, innocent, easily trusting, forgiving, energetic, willing to learn and grow, tenderness of conscious, open, creative, and joyful. Biblically, Jesus said we must embrace Him as a child would (Matt 148:3; Mark 10:14; Luke 18:17). What does this look like? As believers, we must be awed by the Lord, trusting, delighted by Him, and joy filled.

EBONY

Ebony grew up with her siblings and her mom. Her father was not in the picture, so childhood was rough for her single mother. Ebony's mother utilized drugs and alcohol to cover her own pain of grief from losing her mother and from her father's drinking. The saying that hurting people hurt people is relevant in this story. The covering of pain for one brought about emotional pain for another. Ebony had her first child at the age of sixteen when a boy recognized her, and she felt loved. This revealed her low self-esteem and lack of love in her life. She dropped out of high school to raise her son and met another boy at the age of seventeen. They moved in with each other. John was from a Christian home, so this living arrangement brought guilt because they both knew it was not right. Eventually they married. John got saved and took her to church where she became saved also. She shared that she felt relief the minute she accepted Jesus.

While salvation was life-changing for Ebony, the transformation continued when she began to confront the questions and beliefs she held onto from a difficult childhood. She questioned God's love. "If God loved me so much, why did he give me my mom who was an addict? Why did He allow her to treat me the way she did?" Through the confrontation of these questions, forgiveness for her mother resulted. Continued renewal occurred when her belief that "Black people do not get married and love each other" was proven wrong by her in-laws' strong marriage and evident love for each other. She realized she had a choice to make—to not see herself as a victim. Her time in the Word of God revealed she could choose between blessing and a curse, but the choice was hers. Layers of pain needed to be shed for her to find her voice.

Ebony and her husband have now been married for nineteen years, and they have three children. Her transformation was slow, and patience was required to obtain full freedom. However, the goodness of God now presents itself in the ability to take vacations, decorate her home for Christmas, and other fulfilled desires she had as a child that went unmet due to living conditions she endured. Her quote to me was, "I may not be a movie star, but I love my life." Her life is what she had desired as a child. Additionally, Ebony and her husband are the marriage pastors at a church! Only God could bring a belief that black people do not marry or love each other around full circle and use her voice to bring hope and healing to marriages. God is so good!

When our soul is wounded as a child, then it becomes difficult to connect on deep levels. As adults, masks are deployed to cover who we really are so others cannot see us clearly. The problem, we tend to lose ourselves under the façade and become a person who poses as real. You know the act. A person walks into church and someone asks how they are doing, and they respond with, "I'm blessed sister, how are you?" when in reality the person is far from fine, but they suppress, ignore, or dismiss how they feel. Inside they are dying, but they cannot quite put their finger on why. The task—it's time to reclaim the inner child, just like Ebony did.

Our personalities are formed by the time we are around six. If a traumatic event transpires before that age in a person's life, it is woven within his or her foundation. A child grows up thinking there is something wrong with him or herself instead of the problem residing in their environment. Thoughts of, "What is wrong with me?" or "I am defective or unlovable" develop, and the lies of the enemy take root. The view of others and themselves in general are firmly implanted.

The most formative years for social development occur in adolescence from around ages six to twelve. If a painful experience occurs in this timeframe, the ability to trust is hindered, and fear sets in because security is diminished. Take for example children who are bullied. They learn that no one can protect them from the terrorizing person. Now fast forward to when these people are thirty and come into a relationship with Jesus. How easy do you think it will be for them to fully trust the Lord? It will be difficult until they see where He was in that situation. Yes, the Lord was present in that situation.

The most important aspect of this chapter is that until the lies that formed during difficult times are brought to the light, they will remain in the dark with power to keep a person bound. These are the things most people never want to talk about. These are the skeletons in the closet. To be completely free from our past, the core beliefs we hold must realign with the Word of God. We know the Creator of the heavens and all the universe who can shatter previous foundations and give us new perspective.

Most of us know what things trigger our surface wounds. Honestly, we can cope through these situations without much divine intervention. We push through the pain, reason it away, and know that it will soon pass. We may pray about it and ask the Lord to help, but other than being uncomfortable, we manage. The Lord wants to deliver you from these experiences. Only when we stop running from the lies that we believe about ourselves can true freedom result.

Sometimes a wound—the thing you never wanted to talk about, the secret you have never shared with anyone—lurks deep within, and you keep it anchored in darkness to avoid dealing with it. Denial does not stop the situation from being a reality. Perhaps, to get through the situation, you acknowledge what occurred but minimize what happened. You may think you are too far gone or that the event was too bad for healing to be attainable, but is there anything too difficult for God (Jeremiah 32:27)?

Psalm 139 is one I quote and utilize frequently in my own life and in counseling. David identifies in verses 1–6 how the Lord currently knows him:

You have searched me, Lord, and you know me. You know when I sit and when I rise; you perceive my thoughts from afar. You discern my going out and my lying down; you are familiar with all my ways. Before a word is on my tongue you, Lord, know it completely. You hem me in behind and before, and you lay your hand upon me. Such knowledge is too wonderful for me, too lofty for me to attain.

David has such a way with words. He recites that God is aware of him and has knowledge of what David is going to do even before he does it. Better yet, the Lord knows what David is going to say before he even says it. What a powerful picture of a sovereign God who searches His creation. This is surface-level access to the Lord. We are aware that He knows us currently, and we invite Him into this space. For most of us, we feel safe at this level. We can quote Bible verses and have the faith to believe that they relate to us. We shout Hallelujah and mean it. This depth is comfortable and most of the time leaves us unchallenged by His presence.

David does not stop with present actions in our earthly sphere, but he digs deeper in verses 7–12:

Where can I go from your Spirit? Where can I flee from your presence? If I go up to the heavens, you are there; if I make my bed in the depths, you are there. If I rise on the wings of the dawn, if I settle on the far side of the sea, even there your hand will guide me, your right hand will hold me fast. If I say, "Surely the darkness will hide me and the light become night around me," even the darkness will not be dark to you; the night will shine like the day, for darkness is as light to you.

David rationalizes with the Lord that he cannot get away from Him. God is everywhere! Even if David wants to run away, he knows that the Spirit will see. No situation David finds himself in will be out of the purview of the Lord. Difficult positions will even have the light shining on them. This is the intermediate level. There is a knowing in our soul that God is who He says He is. Conviction brings uneasiness, but we relent to His touch on our lives. We must surrender to Him in order to experience His presence. The reality of His love, grace, mercy, and kindness keeps us anchored in Him. We can accept ourselves for the most part on this level. We know we are a work in progress, so we ask Him to change our weaknesses. There are some troublesome points at this layer, but hope and initial freedom beckon us to remain.

David does not stop in Psalm 139 but instead dives headlong in verses 13–18 into the depth of who he is and who God is:

For you created my inmost being; you knit me together in my mother's womb. I praise you because I am fearfully and wonderfully made; your works are wonderful, I know that full well. My frame was not hidden from you when I was made in the secret place, when I was woven together in the depths of the earth. Your eyes saw my unformed body; all the days ordained for me were written in your book before one of them came to be. How precious to me are your thoughts, God! How vast is the sum of them! Were I to count them, they would outnumber the grains of sand—when I awake, I am still with you.

David perceives that his very being was vital to the Lord. God took notice and fashioned him with the exact personality and gifts needed to accomplish that for which the Lord created him. At his very core, there is an awareness that nothing escapes God's plan. David can praise the Lord because since birth everything about him has mattered to the Lord. All his days were already written, and the Lord has genuinely cared for him. David was able to inherently trust the Lord because he knew the Lord, and the Lord knew him—inside and out, from birth to death, and it was okay to be him. This is the intimate level, where deep calls out to deep. They know who they are in Christ. Have you ever seen believers so fixed on Jesus that they rarely lose their peace? Yes, like David, they too may cry out to the Lord for healing or deliverance, but they know that God will answer. Even if God does not answer in the way they would like, they still trust that God is who He says He is. They have such stability that nothing the enemy throws at them sticks. No trial or test moves them from the Lord. Oh, the hope that we all can reach this place. However, not too many Christians reside at this degree.

The most wonderful aspect of this depth is that anyone can achieve it, no matter what their past looks like. What is the secret? Honesty, vulnerability, and humility. Each of us must be honest with ourselves and the Lord. He knows everything anyway. We are not hiding anything from Him. Sure, we think we can at times, but David reminds us that this view is not true. Honesty must begin with our past. We must admit what happened, how we responded to it, and how we currently feel about it. Denial hinders healing.

Next, we must become vulnerable with the Lord and invite Him into our woundedness. This takes trust that God will not harm us further but offer acceptance and love. Humility is vital for healing and can be the most difficult aspect of this process. It's uncomfortable to acknowledge that we have to release anger, hurt, and unforgiveness. We want to demand our rights and vindication. Yet, when we humble ourselves, we give the Lord permission to heal us in His way and timing. Often, people in counseling want the pain to diminish immediately, but the only way to overcome it is by coming face-to-face with it and then laying it down at the foot of the cross.

Most of this book's themes thus far have set the stage for this chapter—the power to transform, perfect peace, more than salvation, forgiveness, life in the Word, and waging war. In order to become vulnerable, we must know God's character. And finally, we must humble ourselves under God and allow His will, His timing, His deliverance, and His healing to have full access in our lives. The acknowledgment that He is God, and we are not, opens the door to intimacy that provides a testimony which, in response to the Psalmist's invitation (Psalm 34:8) says, "I have tasted and seen that the Lord is good!"

The level we live at is dictated by choice, which in turn determines our healing. This statement reminds me of a story in the Bible where Jesus approaches a man at the Pool of Siloam suffering from a disability and asks him, "Do you want to be healed?" (John 5:6). The man comes up with an excuse as to why he has not been healed: "There was no one to help me." How often do we blame others for us not being whole? We may not say it aloud, but in our heart, we declare it. Or we integrate it into ourselves with the thought, "It's just the way I am. I am hopeless and helpless."

This chapter is different in the fact that there is a step-by-step process. This journey has been completed with many people and have found it effective nearly every time. You may need to repeat this with multiple emotions: fear, anger, abandonment, or sadness. In addition, if you have experienced multiple traumatic events, you may need to repeat this process. However, once the very first episode is brought to the light, the others follow—maybe not the same day, but they will unfold. Truth of the Spirit will integrate into the depth of the soul to produce wholeness and healing.

You can go through these steps by yourself or ask a trusted person to be with you. Pray and worship before beginning. Do not over analyze what comes to your mind. You may receive a picture or hear words. Everyone is different. So here is the process.

STEP ONE

Begin in prayer. Ask the Lord what the memory is that He wants to heal. Ask the Lord to bring up in your mind the first time you encountered the issue. The Lord wants to take you back to the very beginning when a stronghold began. You may get a picture of you as a little girl or young boy in a certain room or location. Sit with that for a moment. What is the harm done to you? What do you see or remember about the event? Are there smells, sounds, or anything else you can recall? Are other people present? You can journal the picture or write the words spoken, but if possible, continue to sit until the whole encounter is complete.

STEP TWO

As you reflect on this circumstance, ask the Lord to reveal where He was during that time. Look around you in that memory. Where is Jesus? Is He beside you, across the room, standing above you, where is He? It's okay, allow the tears to flow. You have been angry or felt abandoned, but He was right there with you all along.

STEP THREE

Next, ask the Lord to reveal what lie took root during this moment. Did you hear, "No one could love you; you are dirty; you are worthless; no one can be trusted; love means pain; you could never be forgiven?" What lie came up out of the child within? The devil comes to kill, steal, and destroy (John 10:10). The lie was meant to bind you from being all God had created you to become. However, that is all about to change. What came to your mind? What is the lie that you have believed for years? For some, this may come as a great surprise. For others, you may have already known.

STEP FOUR

Ask the Lord to speak truth to the lie. What is the truth? A Bible verse may come to mind. You may see the Lord hug you, and in your heart the truth penetrates without you even knowing verbally what it is. The bottom line is that the truth sets us free (John 8:32). At this point the initial healing takes place. Acquiesce to the Spirit's moving, and just be still. Concede to the work being done at the core of your inner child.

STEP FIVE

Allow the Spirit to continue to minister to you even when you think you are finished. Rarely do times like this end when you get up. People have texted later in the evening or even a couple of days later and shared how the Spirit continued to reveal things to them. Pick up a journal and begin to write what transpired. This will help you pinpoint what lies you believed and the truth that dispelled them because this same lie may bind you in other situations.

If you experienced nothing, do not feel discouraged. Continue to pray and seek the Lord. Ask Him to search your heart for anything hidden even from you. Isaiah was giving a prophetic word to the people of Israel who were to be freed from captivity: "You have heard these things; look at them all. Will you not admit them? From now on I will tell you new things, of hidden things unknown to you" (Isaiah 48:6). The wound you carry may be buried in a place you have never been or, depending on your age when the trauma occurred, that you have not revisited for decades. Invite a trusted friend to come and pray through this process with you, or find a Christian counselor to walk with you. Do *not* give up! Do not believe the lie that you are unworthy or beyond help.

Continue these steps over and over until you sense a wholeness within you. You may need to repeat these steps a handful of times or just once, depending on circumstances in your past. You may also need to take some time in between repetitions. The importance of your inner child being healed cannot be overstated. We are to be trusting and vulnerable, acknowledging our inability to advance our own will apart from the Lord. If our inner child remains wounded, we cannot attain this level of trust, vulnerability, or dependency. We will be too wrapped up in what we need, want, and feel. We will lack patience. We will allow a sense of self-sufficiency to reign. Our fears will hinder the work God wants to do in us.

I pray you had an encounter with the living God and that the Spirit spoke truth to your heart and the stronghold of lies was broken. Reflect on this chapter multiple times. Do not rush through it or move away too quickly.

What is next? Another choice must be made. Keep pressing.

CHAPTER 9

FREEDOM FROM GRAVE CLOTHES

Our past can only define us if we allow it to.

The interesting aspect about our past is that it contains both positive and negative lessons. We have all learned something from our past that formed us in a positive way. Perhaps we learned determination or resolve, but whatever the healthy outcome was, it formed us. That is what our past does, it molds us into who we currently are. If we retain the negative from the trial we endured, then it will continue to impact our present—and even our future—if we refuse to release it. Yet, for so many people this remains their reality.

Patterns of beliefs and behavior form when people do not let go of their past. Sometimes, it is a conscious choice to remain in bondage; others just did not know how to move forward. People choose not to move beyond their past for many reasons. Because of space, four will be addressed here—fear, not having closure, becoming stuck, and self-pity.

The most common reason people do not move forward is fear. This entails fear of failure, fear of disappointment, fear of other people, fear of being helpless, fear of success, fear of something worse happening, fear of responsibility, fear of attention, fear of rejection, and fear of abandonment. All these different types of fear have one thing in common—people want to remain in control, and to release their past places them in situations where fear of the unknown is triggered.

Have you ever heard of a self-fulfilling prophecy? This is when what you are afraid of happens. Why? Because you are thinking so much about it that you begin to act as though it has already happened, therefore making people respond to you as if it *has* happened, which in turn causes it to actually happen. If you have a fear of abandonment, you may not allow people to come close to you because you are afraid that they will leave you as others have in the past. A person gives up trying to get close to you, so they cease the friendship, which in turn, only solidifies further the fear that people will leave you. This repeated pattern settles deep within core beliefs, and the walls built are impenetrable. You may cry out for friendships and want to get close to another person, but holding onto the past prevents this. Will people leave you in the future? Yes. People are human and can be very selfish, yet you could also be missing out on beautiful relationships because you will not release the fear.

This concept of a self-fulfilling prophecy is biblical. Job 3:25 states, "What I feared has come upon me; what I dreaded has happened to me." Job was lamenting his suffering and recognized that he had thought about the "what if" question beforehand.

Another example of this concept is the fear of failure. This fear prevents a person from stepping out in faith because they are afraid something will not work. Perhaps you went through a divorce or were removed from a ministry position, and you have surrounded yourself with excuses as to why you cannot have another relationship or take another ministry position.

What happens when a person fears other people? Proverbs says the fear of man brings a snare (Proverbs 29:25). A "snare" is something by which one is entangled or impeded, like a trap. When a past situation causes a person to fear rejection or harm, then it impedes his or her ability to accomplish all God created that person to do. The individual becomes paralyzed and entangled instead of moving freely. People pleasing behaviors are a side effect of this, and a person becomes so wrapped up in what others think that he or she no longer knows how to walk in truth.

When a person permits fear to rule, negative situations are likely to happen as a result. What someone attempts to avoid continues to reinforce their fear. Greater sadness and living with regret transpire, which only increases misery and emotional pain. The more a person attempts to avoid pain, the stronger the fear becomes. The best way to address fear is to face it head on.

First John 4:18 reassures us, "There is no fear in love. But perfect love drives out fear, because fear has to do with punishment. The one who fears is not made perfect in love." The Lord does not want us to fear but to abide in His love. His love replaces fear with acceptance, grace, mercy, forgiveness, kindness, and patience. Will people hurt us again? Yes. Will we hurt others? Yes. If everyone was perfect, we would not need

Jesus. We must run to Him when we are wounded and invite Him to heal every fear.

When Timothy struggled with the suffering that Paul experienced, Paul encouraged him by reminding him that God did not give him a spirit of fear, but of power, love, and self-discipline (2 Timothy 1:7). When faced with fear, decide to do whatever it is that is triggering that fear. Do it anyway. Remember, you are a child of God, and His power resides in you. His love fights for you, and only you can make the choice to do it afraid. Say no to fear and yes to God!

Lastly, how did Jesus respond when people attempted to speak of the death of a child to her father? He instructed the father to quit listening to the voices of the people and just believe in Him (Mark 5:36). In order to move beyond our past, we must ignore outside voices—and at times even our own voice—and listen to the One who created us. Allow faith to conquer fear.

The next reason people do not release their past is they do not sense closure. You may feel better about the past but think it remains unsettled in some way. This creates an atmosphere of questioning with the demand for resolution. However, in many events, there will never be closure.

Perception is the main aspect in this example. How you perceive a situation or person will determine your attitude. If you think that the person has not been punished for what they did, then you might attempt to find ways to administer retribution. Has a loved one died, and you were not able to speak with them? You might then feel as though you can never have closure. If you have prayed about a situation, you may still believe that the only closure will result when everything unfolds to your satisfaction. This can entail forgiveness, but it encompasses more.

As humans, we all have expectations regarding what we want resolution to look like, how we want things to unfold. When reality falls short, we tend to blame God or see Him as distant from us. We pray and seek Him to act on our behalf, and then we give Him our plan. When there is silence instead of action on God's part, we tend to analyze and rationalize in our own minds. The need to figure things out overrules our patience to wait on God. Demanding closure becomes the cry of our heart instead of recognizing how God has already moved on our behalf.

One way to overcome the need for closure is to open our spiritual eyes and ears to what the Spirit is currently speaking. Isaiah 43:19 proclaims, "See, I am doing a new thing! Now it springs up; do you not perceive it? I am making a way in the wilderness and streams in the wasteland." We must trust that God knows what He is doing and not rely on our own understanding. Just because the situation does not look like what you wanted it to or think it should does not mean God is not doing a new thing.

I love the story of the walk to Emmaus with the two men and Jesus. Their eyes did not recognize Him, but their hearts burned within them when they talked with Him (Luke 24:32). How many times has the Lord revealed the new thing, and we just did not observe it because we were too caught up in what we thought? We may have sensed something new on the horizon but have never been able to fully grasp what it might be. The only way closure occurs is by trusting the Lord and inviting His Spirit to speak life over death.

The third reason people choose not to move beyond their past is that they just become stuck. It is easy to become focused on just surviving. I can remember in my time of brokenness that I just wanted to make it through each day. When healing began, life returned. However, one night when my husband and I went away to a hotel for a change of scenery, a heaviness returned. "Why, Lord?" resounded in my heart. He revealed that instead of learning to live freely, I was succumbing once again to the survival mindset. Existence was the goal and not victory over my failure.

There is a time where the goal is to make it through the day because the crisis is raging. However, if one is honest, the main brunt of the experience has passed, yet instead of battling to work through all the negative, exhaustion has taken hold.

Have you ever said, "I just feel like I'm existing"? If you have, then quickly turn to the Word of God. Dangers of the world lurk at this point. Some people turn to alcohol, drugs, shopping, pornography, food, gambling, or any other vice in order to feel alive. A mindset that declares, "I am victorious!" must swell within you. The determination to not settle for less than God's best plan for your life needs to grip your heart. God wants to walk with you through the valley of pain and bring you to the other side. There is hope. There is power to bring new strength.

The enemy comes to kill, steal, and destroy, but Jesus came to give us life (John 10:10). The enemy wants to steal your joy and strength. He wants to destroy you by having you so tired that you cannot fight for your future, but Jesus gives life—life in abundance until it overflows! Call out to the Lord for help like the psalmist does: "My soul is weary with sorrow; strengthen me according to your word" (Psalm 119:28). Declare as in Psalm 73:26, "My flesh and my heart may fail, but God is the strength of my heart and my portion forever." Isaiah emphatically proclaims, "God gives strength to the weary and increases the power of the weak" (Isaiah 40:29). Push past the pain and exhaustion, and turn to the Lord.

The last reason people do not move beyond their past is self-pity. There are things you may read that you do not like or agree with, but you must realize that the Lord wants you to move forward. I only ask that you continue to read.

Part of the idea behind self-pity is the thought, "This is too hard." You may have gone through a horrific trauma and do not feel like working through emotional pain. The work it takes to continue may trigger someone to just give up on life or ministry. This is the "Woe is me!" mentality that severs us from the Giver of Life.

Has this thought ever entered your mind: "I did not cause this bad event to happen, so why do I have to deal with the ramifications?" Or what about the thought, "This isn't fair. They left, and I have to deal with the mess." These are two legitimate reasonings, but we know that our thoughts are not God's thoughts.

Pride is at the root of self-pity. Ouch. I know that hurts. It hurt me when the Lord revealed it to me years ago. Pride is anything that sets itself up against God. A person who refuses to let go of their past and forgive has made their pain an idol and placed it above the Lord. That person has focused more on what happened to him or her than on what God instructs them to do.

Merriam-Webster defines "self-pity" as pity for oneself, especially a "self-indulgent dwelling on one's own sorrows or misfortunes."[12] This needs to be broken down. Pity is a feeling of sorrow or compassion for a misfortune. So, people living in self-pity see themselves as having gone through a difficult situation and they feel bad or sorry for themselves. Okay, so what is self-indulgent? Doing or tending to do exactly what one wants, especially when this involves idleness. So, let's put this altogether. Self-pity, then, is when a person who has been through something difficult feels sorry for him or herself and because of this uses it to not have to move forward. That person can seek pity from others in order to gain attention, vengeance, approval, validation, or a number of reactions. Unfortunately, any positive reaction inherently rewards these actions born out of self-pity. The victim mentality gains a foothold. Everyone is out to get them.

I can hear someone saying right now, "But you have no idea what they did to me!" True, it was probably horrible. However, it cannot be changed. Focusing and replaying the situation only serves to keep you miserable and bound. The other person has probably moved on, and you are the one living in the past. Do you want to remain in the despair of the past and how you were wronged and have anger dictate your life? Or are you ready to turn to the Lord and ask Him to help you?

Remember pride is at the root of self-pity. Proverbs 11:2 states, "When pride comes, then comes disgrace, but with humility comes wisdom." The opposite of pride is humility. In order to move forward, one must humble oneself under the Lord by giving Him all the pain and situation and waiting for Him to bring vindication. Romans 12:19 says, "Do not take revenge, my dear friends, but leave room for God's wrath, for it is written: 'It is mine to avenge; I will repay,' says the Lord." God is just, and He will judge accordingly.

Part of the responsibility of a Christian is to let go and allow God to be in charge. Bad things happen to believers just like they happen to unbelievers, and unfortunately, believers are often the cause of a great deal of pain. That is why it hurts so fiercely at times. People are tempted, and they give in to the temptation instead of remaining pure. Sometimes, someone claiming to believe in Jesus uses faith in order to harm us. Additionally, there are always wolves in sheep's clothing—people who really do not believe but they say they do just to harm us.

One day Jesus called his disciples and a crowd to himself and said to them "Whoever wants to be my disciple must deny themselves and take up their cross and follow me. For whoever wants to save their life will lose it, but whoever loses their life for me and for the gospel will save it" (Mark 8:34–35). Truly, we all have our crosses to bear—pasts that caused pain, hurt, and woundedness. We must yield up the pain to follow Jesus.

Fear, needing closure, feeling stuck, and self-pity must be surrendered. All of it. The only way forward is through letting go.

TAKE OFF THE GRAVE CLOTHES

I already shared that when I became stuck during a time of brokenness in my life, the Lord revealed to me that I was just surviving instead of embracing life. He next led me to John 11 and the story where Lazarus was raised from the dead. Jesus had spoken with Martha and Mary about their brother living again. Let's pick up at John 11:40–44:

> *Then Jesus said, 'Did I not tell you that if you believe, you will see the glory of God?' So they took away the stone. Then Jesus looked up and said, 'Father, I thank you that you have heard me. I knew that you always hear me, but I said this for the benefit of the people standing here, that they may believe that you sent me.' When he had said this, Jesus called in a loud voice, 'Lazarus, come out!' The*

dead man came out, his hands and feet wrapped with strips of linen, and a cloth around his face Jesus said to them, 'Take off the grave clothes and let him go.'

You may be feeling right now that you have been dead inside—dead emotionally and spiritually, but life has come!

It took the act of believing that Lazarus would be raised from the dead. Both Martha and Mary believed that Jesus could and would give him new life—maybe not in the way they thought He would, but nevertheless they believed. Do you believe that God can bring new life to you? Jesus reveals that He is the way, the truth, and the life (John 14:6). God can and does bring new life. This whole story is about Jesus and the coming resurrection for all people.

Lazarus was called out. He could not give himself new life but was completely dependent on God. You, too, must depend on God to revive you. He is calling you forth right now. Do not live in your past any longer. Do not allow insecurities from years of bullying keep you bound. Can you hear the Lord beckoning you?

The most important part of the story for this book is that the grave clothes had to be removed. When Lazarus died, he was wrapped in burial clothes. These would have been placed around his head covering his eyes and ears, and around the rest of his body, including his arms and legs. These wraps kept him from quickly decaying, in a sense, to protect him from the effects of death, but they kept him bound.

This point cannot be missed. We are resurrected with Christ when we become believers. However, situations and difficulties bring death to us, and we are wrapped in grave clothes. Sometimes we keep them on to prevent further harm. The Lord is calling us out from the past, though, and He yearns for the grave clothes to be removed. This is where most people stop. They come from the grave site, but they do not remove the clothes because they feel better since the circumstance is over. Do not stop! Allow others to help you remove the grave clothes. God did His part by bringing new life. It is now up to you to ask the Lord to help you remove things that resulted from your pain. New life has arrived!

What happens if we choose not to take off the grave clothes? Bondage remains. Lazarus was able to walk out of the grave, but can you imagine what he looked like trying to walk with his arms and legs wrapped up? Picture a mummy taking little, tiny steps, unable to move freely. This is what we look like when we refuse to remove the clothes. We walk around stumbling, not moving very fast, if at all. People see we are bound and hindered in our movement. We can identify people in this state. They are the ones with a calling on their life, but they never have open doors. They have such potential, but something is always standing in the way. They are the ones at the altar every week asking for prayer for the same issue, yet they never seem to improve.

When a person chooses to remain in their past, it causes them to become selfish and self-centered because it restricts their movement. Negative emotions bind their ability to reach out and help others. Sure, on the surface they appear okay because of the mask they wear. However, decisions made must travel through the pain before an actual plan is derived. Do these thoughts sound familiar: "I have to protect myself. I have to take care of me because no one else will. What happens if I make a mistake?"

What does this look like in my life? If I had not taken off the fear of failure, this book would not have been written. If I would not have taken off self-sufficiency, I would not be able to trust the Lord and accept His help. What does it look like in your life?

Jesus said in John 8:32, 36, "Then you will know the truth, and the truth will set you free. So if the Son sets you free, you will be free indeed." It is time to let go. Jesus is calling you to cast off your fears. He is asking you to release disappointment. It is time to walk in freedom. Complete freedom!

Paul admonishes believers in Galatians 5:1, "It is for freedom that Christ has set us free. Stand firm, then, and do not let yourselves be burdened again by a yoke of slavery." Paul was telling the people in Galatia not to allow others' viewpoints to cause them to backslide. Do you hear those same words now? Do not permit the voices of others, the enemy, or even your own voice to keep you bound. If you need help, ask for it. Remember, Lazarus could not remove his own burial clothes.

Not only was Lazarus's walking hindered by clothes, but his ability to see and hear was also hindered. Obviously, he heard Jesus and the power of the Spirit while dead, and so can we. Can you imagine, though, if the clothes would have remained over his eyes and ears? This would have greatly changed his ability to see where he needed to walk or hear what he needed to do. When the Lord brings new life, we must decide to remove the old in order to see clearly and hear clearly. Otherwise, we will be viewing our future through the lens of past wounds. Yet, just like in the case of Lazarus, we cannot remove our past on our own. Our pain needs divine intervention to be detached.

What does this look like? Always feeling as though you must prove yourself in order for people to recognize your calling. Yes, I did that for years. This was miserable. What does it look like in your life? Could it be that you decreased time spent reading the Word or being still with the Lord because you know you have not been obedient in stepping out into that new ministry? Do you feel tied up in knots every time you talk with a leader because you second guess everything you said? Have you stopped dreaming with God and instead settled into complacency?

It is time for the grave clothes to come off. It is time for the healing salve of the Lord to flow to the depths of your being and cover all emotional pain, fears, and wounds. Face your fears, change your perspective, pray for strength, and quit feeling sorry for yourself. Go ahead. Stand up right where you are. Picture a heavy coat that is weighing you down. Now, see that coat falling to the ground through the power of the Holy Spirit. Allow the Lord to pull it off. Can you sense the weight is removed from your shoulders? No. Keep replaying this through your mind until it takes hold. Visualize the grave clothes being removed from your eyes and ears. Can you hear the still small voice better? Can you see clearer the path before you? Wait. Be patient. You will.

CHAPTER 10

LIFE WITHOUT LIMITS

"Am I now trying to win the approval of human beings, or of God?
Or am I trying to please people? If I were still trying to please people,
I would not be a servant of Christ"
—Galatians 1:10

Where does the desire to please people instead of the Lord come from? It stems from the fear of people. "People" can represent a boss, likes on Facebook, denominational leadership, women in a life group, or even our family. This fear keeps us from following the Lord or being obedient to what He instructs us to do because of what other people will think or how they will respond. Proverbs 29:25 reminds us, "Fear of man will prove to be a snare, but whoever trusts in the Lord is kept safe." What is a snare? Basically, it is a trap. The enemy of our soul wants to ensnare us to keep us confined. This prevents us from fully living in freedom and thus stifles life.

What are some circumstances that happen in our lives to create this bondage? A history of sexual abuse, domestic violence, lack of security from a chaotic household growing up, abandonment, lack of financial resources, severe rejection, bullying, or several other situations trigger intense insecurities and an inability to trust our own judgement, therefore we seek approval from others. When others tell us we are okay, then we "feel" okay. It is the need to be validated that presses upon our hearts. Whatever occurred in the past to cause us to be afraid of others must be dealt with to have a life with no limits.

We all want to feel significant. When there is a fear of people, the gaze has gone to those around us and the world to determine our significance, instead of the One who created us. We buy into the lies of the devil, our parents, or the person who harmed us, the statements, "You will never amount to anything!", "You are stupid.", "You are not man enough.", "You are a woman.", or any other voices that degrade or dismantle a belief in who God says we are. As scripture states we are children of God and joint heirs with Christ (Romans 8:17).

What does cowering to people look like? Like any other concept, there are examples that range from daily decisions to life altering actions. We alter plans so others do not get upset with us, yet we resent them for our decision. We remain hidden at home instead of stepping out in faith because "what will people think?" We allow the opinion of others to keep us from speaking up about Jesus because we might be rejected from the "popular" club. We might be killed or ridiculed because we go against family tradition of another religion.

What does it look like in your life? In my life, it meant remaining quiet while sitting with other ministers because I felt inadequate or had nothing to offer. Or the opposite, it meant me trying to prove myself by always talking about my accomplishments which pushed people away and left me feeling even more rejected, which triggered a cycle of self-doubt.

This was an area of struggle for me for years. Not only did I have past issues growing up that allowed this fear to take root, but then when I stepped into ministry, I had a person in leadership tell me I should choose a different fellowship to obtain ordination. He informed me that I already had three strikes against me—I was a woman, I was an evangelist, and I did not grow up in the fellowship. This was ripe ground for bondage. From that day forward, the need to prove myself to others resulted. Oh, how thankful I am the Lord can transform us! Dr. Melody Palm, one of my professors while obtaining my Doctor of Ministry, once said, "When you have nothing to prove, you have nothing to lose." Those words rang true in my heart and the stronghold was acknowledged and then given to the Lord. I pray these same words begin to ring true in you.

Part of this chapter comes from a time of devotion with the Lord. This will help us arrive at the heart of the matter. Let me set the stage: I was just beginning to read the book of John and came across John 1:38 where Jesus asked Nathaniel, "What are you seeking?" (ESV).

Immediately, the still, small quiet voice asked me the same question—"Kristi, what are you seeking?" (This question was not referring to salvation and went beyond the Christianese of You, Lord. I seek You.)

I attempted to read on, but my mind kept returning to the question. I finished the chapter and began to answer the question. "Lord, I want to do Your will."

"Why do you want to do My will?"

"For notoriety!" bubbled to the top of my thoughts. "Oh no, Lord, could there be any ounce of truth in this?"

"Kristi, this is only the partial truth. This has to go but keep answering."

"So that others may know You", arose in my heart. I felt good about this answer.

"But why should people know Me?"

By this time I was astonished at this conversation. I had never had such an experience such as this. Yet I went on to answer, "Because You are the Light of the world. You bring freedom from sin and death. You bring uncompromising and uncontaminated love."

"Yes. Why is this so vital?"

"Because without You, Lord, we are dead." There it was. I shouted out, "LIFE! I seek life." I sensed the Spirit fill the room and begin to unfold His desire for His children to please Him and the reason "Why."

The information below is not new. There has been no revelation to me alone. However, I hope that it is presented in such a way that brings a renewing of your mind. Lord, may the truth You reveal penetrate the core of our being.

What does life provide? Life provides freedom from death, sin, bondages, and strongholds. Life also provides rest. Rest from striving and trying to accomplish tasks in our own strength, including salvation. Rest also includes trusting the Lord to direct instead of us having to figure everything out on our own. Life also provides joy. A deep satisfaction with the focus on all that we are thankful for. Lastly, life brings the promise of eternity. The knowledge that earth is not our ultimate home brings hope in a better tomorrow.

Only the Lord brings life. Jesus said He is the way, the truth, and the Life (John 14:6). The Lord said He came to bring life and life abundantly (John 10:10). There is no other way to arrive at the fullness of life that a belief in Christ provides.

Before salvation we only knew death. We were going to die, and that is it. We were dead in our transgressions. Sin makes us dead. All people sin, so all are dead. Only through the removal of sin can we truly live. The death of Christ removes our sin because His resurrection conquered death and brought eternal life.

As a result, the new life afforded to us relinquishes sin that at one time had a hold on us. Our desire is to live freely in the light and have intimate fellowship with the One who purchased our freedom. We owe the Lord our very life. Yet, He does not want us to "feel" like we have no other choice, but He wants us to "choose" Him because we recognize His sacrifice, love, and holiness.

Gratefulness arises within us when we meditate on the fact that we have been delivered from death into life. This was purchased through the cross. We can now live and move and have our being because Christ purchased "life" for us. Without this extreme cost of His love, we would never have it. It is only through Christ's steadfast love and faithfulness that we can truly live.

So why would we want people to look at us, pat us on the back, and put us on pedestals when we do something for Jesus? We should not. Yet time after time, there is a longing for recognition if insecurities exist. Now, being encouraged by others to keep going and not give up is not what I am referring to here. I am talking about the need for others to say something positive or the trip home entails strong feelings of failure because the acclaim did not occur.

We need to point people to Jesus because He gave us life.

We did nothing to deserve this life.

We did nothing to create our life.

We only receive life through the gift of grace.

If we have done nothing, we have no claim to the notoriety of it. Therefore, we have no right to seek the spotlight or expansion of our own name. We should take no thanks for anything. People should remember the experience with Jesus through whom life is given more than our name.

Furthermore, if God gives life, only He can take it away. This includes the breath in our lungs and the death of our physical bodies. This includes the fear of people. Jesus said to His disciples not to be afraid of those who can harm the body but be afraid of the One who can destroy both soul and body (Matthew 10:28).

If only the Lord gives life, why do we fear those who can do nothing to us? Why do we give people the power to make us miserable instead of living in freedom, rest, and joy? Yes, people may take the last breath from a person, but they cannot take their "life." This reminds me of missionaries who serve the Lord in dangerous areas or people who are martyred for their faith. There is truth that people can kill our bodies. Let me clarify for a moment, I am not addressing the fear of literal danger or relationships of violence. Should a person stay in an abusive marriage until they are killed? Absolutely not! Please do not allow the father of all lies to turn this around right now and attempt to sway you to not utilize wisdom and leave certain situations or circumstances.

If we truly seek life, the realization that it has already been given and cannot be taken away must surface. No one can take anything away from us, only we can give it up. Even Jesus said He lays down His life and no one could kill Him unless He laid it down (John 10:18).

If we choose to live in freedom from sin and worldly ways, with joy in the Lord and the recognition that we are loved beyond measure, and rest in knowing that God is in control of our lives, then nothing can hinder us. We can rest because we do not have to work to become saved because Jesus already paid the full price. We can rest also because God fights for us. Again, no eternal reward can be taken from us (John 10:28). We need to rest in His love and plan for our lives (Jeremiah 29:11). Rest in the knowledge that no good thing will He withhold from us (Luke 12:32). Rest in knowing He is with us. He lives inside of us.

Again, no one can take this away from us. We can only give it up. Today we must choose life. We must choose to walk in freedom, rest, and joy. Knowing the truth of what Jesus died and rose to offer us. Knowing He is who He says He is and that we are who He says we are.

We do as He leads because we love Him and are thankful that He died for us—the wretched sinners we were. We do what He instructs so others can experience this same life and live more abundantly than they can ever know. Why would we want people to not know this life that lives inside of us? I remember how miserable I was and how free I am now.

You might know Jesus as your Savior, but are you free? Free to be who God has created you to be? Are you free to do what God has created, called, and anointed you to accomplish? Or are you wrapped up and bound by the approval and fame from others? People who have done nothing, are nothing, and can never do anything worthy of life?

We can respect, love, and help others, but we can never allow them to take the place of Savior in our lives. This is the root of the fear of people. Thinking that another person has the power over us. The only power they have is what we give them in our mind. Yes, they can take our physical life, but not eternal life. Yes, they can make our lives more difficult, but they cannot take our freedom, rest, or joy. They only take what we give them.

Choose this day to not give your life away to another person. I choose today to walk in the life that Jesus died to give me, and so can you, life that only He gives and has the power to take.

Intimidation, threats, rejection, taunting, bullying, or any other negative behavior has no power over us when we get to the depth of our being that only God is the giver of life. That if we are rejected by a person, God accepts us and that will NEVER change. Can situations and circumstances be life altering? Yes. Are they emotionally painful? Yes. But we should never bow to a person when the Giver of life lives in us. The same power that resurrected our Lord and Savior lives in each of us right now. Will you allow that power to rise within you to strengthen you? Will you allow the Spirit to comfort you when needed? Will you allow that same Spirit to give you wisdom when words are needed? Will you allow that same Spirit to direct you even in the face of opposition?

If we live for God, then we do not live for humans. Oh, the freedom this brings. If we live to please God, then pleasing others does not become part of the equation. Of course, I am not referring to give and take in relationships.

Can we please God and do it in a loving way? Absolutely. Paul encourages the people at Ephesus to speak the truth in love (Ephesians 4:15). Even Jesus informed His disciples that people will know they follow Him because of their love (John 13:35). We must not become hard hearted to fully live and please God. On the contrary, our heart is softened towards others because we know we have done nothing to deserve life. We know it is only by grace that we can even breathe.

So why would we judge others? I am not referring to unbelievers here. I am referencing Christians judging Christians for everyday issues, not even biblical truths. Why do we bring condemnation on those who do not look like us, act like us, or respond like us? The answer, because differences threaten our stability and unhinge the view of ourselves. If our beliefs are challenged, then that means we are not okay. In order for us to continue living in our own little worlds, then our idea of things has to remain unshaken. Judging others placates this fear.

Oh, brothers and sisters, if only we could grasp the love it took for Jesus to go to the cross and remain on the cross. He could have saved Himself and come down off the cross as people were taunting Him to do (Matthew 27:42). But He chose love instead. Lord, may we too choose love instead of pride. May we choose love instead of a judgmental attitude. Oh Lord, may we choose love over a critical spirit. All these examples reveal pride and the inner heart of a wounded person.

Once we grasp what the cross actually did, then we can give up our own guilt, shame, and pride and completely surrender. See, the fear of humans is about our own insecurities and pride.

We find it difficult to admit it is not about us at all. Once we grasp this truth, the fear of people diminishes. If we realize there is nothing we can do to earn life, then we recognize no one else can either. We are all in the same boat. Lost and going to hell without the intervention of a blood sacrifice. Well, thanks be to God for sending Jesus, His Son, to deliver all of us from sin and death.

Humans did not give life; so they cannot take it.

Humans did not call you; so they cannot dictate your progress.

Humans do not give you power; so do not give them the power to rule over you.

May the prayer of all our hearts be like my dear friend Jamie's prayer, "Lord expand our ability to withstand pain." Not suffering from life, but pain brought on because we are Christ followers. Intolerance to pain tends to make us give up our life to please people. But may we press fully into the Lord when situations do cause heartache and not allow them to bring a stronghold of fear. It is only then will we experience a life without limits.

The picture of a person with handcuffs breaking crosses my mind right now. Is that you? Has the power of people been released from your soul? What's next then? When transformation is in process, the need to make choices remains heightened. How do we turn our ashes from the past into beauty? There must be an exchange.

CHAPTER 11

THE EXCHANGE

*"There is no passion to be found in settling for a life
that is less than the one you are capable of living."*
—Nelson Mandela

You have been going through a period of emotional, mental, and spiritual sifting thus far in this book. Your faith has been tested, your emotions pushed to the limit, and at times your mind was even on overload. Yet here you are still. You are stronger than ever. Your strength, though it appears nonexistent at times, runs deep. You are more humble now than ever. You have reflected on life in general and have gone higher in your spiritual journey with the Lord.

Do you recognize the connection between how your relationship with the Lord has gone deeper when there has been open and honest evaluation of self? This is how God works. When we feel broken or struggling, He reaches down, grabs hold of us, and lifts us up. We rise out of the pit, and He places our feet on the Rock. Our foundation is built on solid ground—Him.

Years ago, I spoke at an AGLOW women's meeting in St. Louis, Missouri and enjoyed it so much that I returned the next month. That evening, after the main speaker shared her message, she said she felt like she had a word from the Lord for a few of us. While she was giving a word of prophecy to someone on the opposite side, suddenly, the Spirit rushed upon me. I knew something was about to happen, but being new to the Pentecostal faith, was not quite sure what it was. The lady on the platform looked straight at me and began prophesying as tears flowed freely down my cheeks. I do not remember her name, but will never forget what she spoke. Part of the message entailed, "God has picked you up. Even when you did not think you could go on, God picked you up."

God has been accomplishing the same thing for you as you read Transformed. He has picked you up, whether from off the floor or from deep within a pit, and has been reconstructing the way you think, feel, and act. This is a process, but it cannot stop here. There is still more to come. You are in the homestretch but need to take one last step. It is called an *exchange*.

Isaiah 61:1–3 states,

The spirit of the Lord God is upon me, because the Lord has anointed me to proclaim good news to the poor. He has sent me to bind up the brokenhearted, to proclaim freedom for the captives and release from darkness for the prisoners, to proclaim the year of the Lord's favor and the day of vengeance of our God, to comfort all who mourn, and provide for those who grieve in Zion—to bestow on them a crown of beauty instead of ashes, the oil of joy instead of mourning, and a garment of praise instead of a spirit of despair. They will be called oaks of righteousness, a planting of the Lord for the display of his splendor.

This passage in Isaiah has such importance in my life, as this is the Scripture with which the Lord called me into ministry. As I reflect upon my life, it was exactly what I needed—to exchange my past for who He had ordained me to be. But something needed to happen deep within before I could walk on a platform and preach to the multitudes. What was it that needed to happen? I needed to exchange my past, my pain, my failures, and my weaknesses, for who He had created, called, and anointed me to become. The same holds true with you. This is a divinely appointed time in your life right now. Do not rush beyond this moment, but instead recognize it as the key to a pivotal point where transformation fully transpires.

In this passage, Isaiah was reminding the Israelites in bondage that one was coming to rescue them. We know that One is Jesus. As Jesus recites this verse in Luke 4:18 and says, "Today this Scripture has been fulfilled in your hearing" (v. 21). The Spirit of God was upon Jesus to lift up out of brokenness, sin, and death to all who would come to Him. He was anointed to heal the brokenhearted, to proclaim liberty, and set the captives free. Friends, that is you and me. But His work in us continues beyond freedom to favor. What does this look like in our lives?

Jesus came to comfort all who mourn. We must give Him our grief and pain to receive comfort. Jesus came to give us beauty, but we must exchange the ashes of our past to receive it. When we give Him our mourning, sadness, depression, or fears, then He gives us joy. When we give Him feelings of hopelessness, then He gives us a garment of praise.

What happens during this exchange? When we forfeit everything negative and painful in our lives, then we are called "oaks of righteousness" (Isaiah 61:3) so we may display God's splendor. How beautiful is that!

To be completely restored and healed, we must give God everything. He desires that you exchange your brokenness for all He is. It is tempting to quit before this point. If we have suffered for a while, we become complacent in our trial because of its familiarity. Pain becomes a friend, and we adjust to it. It is not uncommon for apathy, complacency, and idleness to keep us from initiating the exchange. In some counseling sessions, people identify with their pain as who they are and become terrified of expectations placed on them by themselves and others if they choose to take a step forward. Here are a few comments often heard: "When I give this all up, what happens if I fail at being me? What happens if I fail God and fall back into my old life? What if people expect more from me now, and I am not able to produce?"

If you relate to these thoughts, know that God desires more for your life. If you were honest right now, you would admit that something within you longs for more also. You yearn for what is true. This is an opportunity to remove the mask you have been wearing in front of others and allow them to see the real you—not the person engulfed with pain, but the one God created to be vulnerable and in community with fellow believers. The fear of the unknown keeps many people chained to their pain, but you have made it this far. Why not keep putting one foot in front of the other and walk onward?

What does it mean to become an "oak of righteousness" (Isaiah 61:3)? It means God gets the glory and praise when we stand in right relationship with Him. Others witness His power, His glory, His grace, and His love in our lives when transformation progresses. If someone who knew me long ago would see me now, they would immediately understand that it was only God who could have changed me. My own sister states that out of all three of us girls, I was the least expected one to preach the gospel. That is the truth—only God could change my heart and life.

Jeremiah 29:11 encourages us, "For I know the plans I have for you, declares the Lord, plans to prosper you and not to harm you, plans to give you hope and a future." This Scripture was spoken to the Israelites at a time when they were in exile in Babylon. God wanted to do amazing things through the Israelites, to shine the light of Jesus, and He wants to do the same thing in your life. It may feel difficult to see what the future holds, but we know Who holds it.

I encourage you, push one last time. For those who have gone through labor, you know that toward the end it is those last pushes where the birth results. You feel exhausted and a mess. You are gritting your teeth. The doctor says, "One more push! I can see the head. It will all be over with one more push!" I am cheering you on right now. *Push!* Push past this one last hurdle. Lay it all down at the cross, and walk away with beauty, joy, and praise so the light of Christ may shine through you.

MOLDED INTO HIS IMAGE

Philippians 1:6 states, "Being confident of this, that he who began a good work in you will carry it on to completion until the day of Jesus Christ." Isn't it good to know that God does not leave us in our messes but will complete healing in us? God did not bring you out of your mess without giving you a ministry. He does not bring you through your pain without giving you purpose. We overcome by the blood of the Lamb and the word of our testimony (Revelation 12:11).

Paul writes about the fruit of the Spirit being love, joy, peace, kindness, goodness, faithfulness, gentleness, and self-control

(Galatians 5:22–23). His presence works these characteristics in us throughout our lives, especially when we make the journey of transformation. Right now you have more love for God because you have experienced it at a deeper level. Joy is rising within you because you comprehend that your Redeemer lives. You have more peace because nothing has come close to the storm you went through, and yet here you stand. You have made it through. You have more patience because you have learned how to wait on the Lord. You have more kindness because you tend to look at what another person is experiencing through the lens of compassion, not judgment. You exhibit more goodness because you know what it feels like to hurt. You remain more committed because you know the One who has proved Himself faithful to you. Your gentleness with others has increased because you know the feeling of brokenness. You walk in more self-control because you realized you *had* no control, and you learned how to exercise restraint instead of just reacting.

This is where you begin to observe beauty in brokenness. When you trade in your ashes, people notice a difference in you. Your speech, behavior and commitments change. As I discussed at the beginning of this book, what felt like an end in your life is becoming the springboard into your destiny. God does not waste anything we go through but will turn it into good for us and for others when we give it to Him in exchange for His glory (Romans 8:28).

I would not be where I am today had God not used trials to mold me into who I am. I would have run for the hills had God not prepared me along the way. That is how good God is. He will use our ashes to make us more beautiful to promote His Kingdom. Life is all about His plan, not ours. God has always been preparing you for something greater. You were born with a purpose; He has placed you on a journey since the day you were born. The exchange of your ashes to receive His beauty is just one step closer to freedom. The enemy has attempted to destroy you, but God has sustained you for such a time as this.

Therefore, since we have been justified through faith, we have peace with God through our Lord Jesus Christ, through whom we have gained access by faith into this grace in which we now stand. And we boast in the hope of the glory of God. Not only so, but we also glory in our sufferings, because we know that suffering produces perseverance; perseverance, character; and character, hope. And hope does not put us to shame, because God's love has been poured into our hearts through the Holy Spirit, who has been given to us. —Romans 5:1–5

No matter what you have gone through, God loves you. You have reason to rejoice because of His glory. Someday we all will live in His presence. The joy of that day eagerly spurs us on with joy and hope for a better tomorrow when we will see our Savior face-to-face.

Your character has been molded, formed, and refined. Your ability to move beyond speaks volumes to those around you who have observed the whole process. You have not been perfect or done everything correctly, but isn't it good to know that Christ's death has already removed all that away also?

Right now I implore someone to continue to push. You are reading this, and you think being a Christian is too hard—or that life is too hard—and you just want to give up. Your thought is, "If it is going to be like this, then I don't want to be part of it." You know what that "it" is—perhaps a marriage, a ministry, or even a job. Keep pushing and keep reading.

Philippians 3:13–14 states, "Brothers and sisters, I do not consider myself yet to have taken hold of it. But this one thing I do: forgetting what is behind and straining toward what is ahead, I press on toward the goal to win the prize for which God has called me heavenward in Christ Jesus." What had Paul not received yet? He was referring to not having confidence in the flesh but having confidence for Christ's sake. Laying down everything for Jesus will gain a superior prize. The same holds true when we make the exchange. When we let go of what is behind and press forward into the future, He removes the chains and sets us free!

How do we make the exchange? What does it look like? First, let me give you an example. If your spouse left you, you would have to trust someone else in a relationship again and not shut people out. If you experience a crushing blow in ministry, you would need to step out again when prompted by the Spirit. If you suffer from a medical issue, making the exchange means still having joy and lifting the spirits of others all around you. In my life, it meant spending quiet time with God again and then stepping out in obedience, squelching the fear of failure.

EXCHANGE IN THE LIFE OF DAVID

In 1 Samuel 16, the prophet Samuel was instructed to anoint a new king:

> But the Lord said to Samuel, 'Do not consider his appearance or his height, for I have rejected him. The Lord does not look at the things people look at. People look at the outward appearance, but the Lord looks at the heart. ... So Samuel took the horn of oil and

anointed him in the presence of his brothers, and from that day on
the Spirit of the Lord came powerfully upon David. —vv. 7, 13

What an awesome scene! David goes on to slay Goliath in 1 Samuel 17, fight many battles, and conquer many enemies, having great success. Unfortunately, the story takes a drastic turn, and his reality completely changes. David ends up running for his life for many years. He hides out in caves and is not treated like a king. He survives off the land, not palace food. King Saul hates him and wants him dead.

This may resonate with you right now. Maybe you married the woman of your dreams, and life was good, but something happened and shifted your whole life. You were perfect with two kids, a good job, and a white picket fence. Then cancer happened. Then the abuse began. Then an affair occurred. Then a child died. Whatever it was, something ensued, and your life has never been the same. The thought, "It isn't supposed to be like this," surfaces as the pain sets in.

Even though it took years to unfold, God was faithful in raising up David as king. David reigns in Judah for seven years and six months; then it gets even better. In second Samuel 5:3–4 we learn that David is anointed king over Israel. He is thirty years old when he begins his forty-year reign. Can you imagine being anointed king as a teenager and then not becoming king until you were thirty? Imagine the years that passed and how David could have given up. But he did not.

How did David make the exchange from unmet dreams, rejection, betrayal, and confusion? David remained pure before the Lord and continued to give God his pain. Yes, it took time for the promise to become king. However, it was all worth it. In the Psalms, we observe that David did not push away his pain but submitted it to the Lord. He says, "Why are you downcast, oh my soul?" (Psalm 42:5). Sometimes David just prays and asks the Lord to get rid of his enemies. The point? David made the exchange by continually going to God and laying his struggles at God's feet instead of taking matters into his own hands.

One time, David could have killed King Saul who had been hunting him, but instead, he cut off a corner of the king's garment and reminded Saul that he meant him no harm (1 Samuel 24). In 1 Samuel 26:9–11, David tells his men not to touch God's anointed when they go into Saul's camp once again and not to harm him.

The exchange is about laying down what we want to see happen to the other person or what we want to see in our own life—and embracing the Lord's plan. David tells Abishai not to touch the Lord's anointed (v. 9). It is not the Lord's plan for us to gather as many people to our side to justify our own behaviors. We are to lay everything at the foot of the cross and wait for God to move. That is how David continued to make the exchange.

The New Testament quotes the Lord as calling David "a man after my own heart" (Acts 13:22). What a powerful lesson. Yes, David went on to become king, but for the promise to be fulfilled he had to continually exchange his harmful emotions for God's plan. The trials are for God's best.

EXCHANGE IN THE LIFE OF RUTH

What a powerful story of love and redemption which unfolds in the book of Ruth. We come on the scene with Ruth's father-in-law, brother-in-law, and own husband having died. Ruth must have felt heartbroken. Overwhelming loss triggered her to grasp ahold of Naomi and not let go. Ruth refused to leave Naomi's side even when prospects of a future were brighter if she stayed in her own country, Moab. Could Ruth have been experiencing a fear of abandonment? Perhaps she was thinking, "Not one more loss!" Yet, she determinedly moved forward.

In chapter 1 of this biblical narrative, Ruth and Naomi return alone to Israel and find favor. Ruth exchanges her grief for hard work and sheer grit. The Scripture even states that she did not take many breaks, and she worked long hours. Could she have been working hard to forget her pain? We will never know the inner thoughts of Ruth, but we do see her devotion to her mother-in-law throughout the story. Ruth remains so focused on taking care of her mother-in-law that she approaches her kinsman redeemer in order to have provision for the rest of her life.

Ruth exchanged self-pity to bring hope to others. Boaz even commented on Ruth's character when he noticed she did not pursue a younger man. Ruth was set on helping others and not remaining in her grief.

Could this be what you need today? Have you experienced a tragic loss that you need to exchange for hope of a better tomorrow? Does the Lord need to turn your mourning into joy? Let Him turn the ashes of the past into a beautiful life that displays His character of compassion toward others.

EXCHANGE IN THE LIFE OF JOSEPH

God gave great and powerful dreams to Joseph. However, he shared too much with his brothers, who were already jealous because their father loved him the most. Provoked by jealousy, they planned the unspeakable—to kill him. As things turned out, though, they sold him to a passing caravan (Genesis 37). How do you think Joseph felt? Do you think he thought, "This is not how this is supposed to go. Why is this happening?" God had placed a call on Joseph's life, yet he was sold into slavery.

Even through this trial, though, God's favor rested on Joseph because he kept his purity and eyes on the Lord. In the lavish lifestyle of Potiphar, God was with him, and Joseph was promoted. Maybe now his dreams would become reality—but no, he was wrongly accused and sent to prison only to find himself in a pit once again. Yet God remained with him through the interpreting of dreams for others. Once again, though, he was forgotten by others. I do not know about you, but at this point I may have felt bitter, resentful, even apathetic toward God, but Joseph did not. Finally, he was released from prison for interpreting Pharaoh's dream. Imagine God using something given as a gift to you, only to require you to use it for someone else's blessing. Because Joseph exchanged selfish ambition for God's plan, though, he was promoted to second in command of Egypt (Genesis 41:41–45).

Here the story really unfolds. There is a great famine in the land, and Joseph's brothers go to Egypt to obtain food to eat. Joseph recognizes his brothers when they enter, but they do not recognize him. Joseph could have easily sent his brothers away in anger, but here is how Joseph responds to his brothers in Genesis 45:4–8:

> Then Joseph said to his brothers, "Come close to me." When they had done so, he said, "I am your brother Joseph, the one you sold into Egypt! And now, do not be distressed and do not be angry with yourselves for selling me here, because it was to save lives that God sent me ahead of you. For two years now there has been famine in the land, and for the next five years there will be no plowing and reaping. But God sent me ahead of you to

preserve for you a remnant on earth and to save your lives by a great deliverance."

Powerful! How could Joseph forgive his brothers, Potiphar's wife, the cup bearer, and the baker? Because he exchanged pain for promise. What did the exchange look like in Joseph's life? He kept his eyes on God and not on his surroundings. Joseph held onto the promises of God through whatever circumstances transpired. He trusted in the plan of God.

God will promote you when it is His time. People have not been standing in your way. God has called you, and He will promote you, but it is all in His timing. God could not promote Joseph until it was time to prepare for the drought. The way to release your ashes is to completely trust God. He has an exact plan for your life that *will* unfold if you partner with Him. This is when your life becomes beautiful to others. You can walk in peace and trust even amid uncertainty and adverse events.

EXCHANGE IN THE LIFE OF ESTHER

What a heart wrenching story of Queen Esther. It begins when the current queen refuses to dance in front of drunk men and is banned from the king's presence. The king's advisers had a great plan to distract the king with another woman. The story becomes one of sex trafficking. Esther is minding her own business and living her life when she is abruptly kidnapped and taken for the pleasure of the king because of her beauty. She goes through a purification process and is then presented to the king to "be with" him. Esther finds favor with the king, and he chooses her.

What did Esther go through during this time? As a female, I would be angry—being treated as an object for the pleasure of others rather than as a human being. The fact that she was raised by her uncle Mordecai leads us to believe she was orphaned. Was she already suffering from grief when she was taken? Did this process lead to depression or anxiety?

We see Esther gain favor with the king's handlers. Even when all that unravels, she keeps her grace and dignity as much as possible. She even focuses on what the king would have desired. Could it be possible that this trauma had brainwashed her into thinking it was a favor to her to be chosen?

As the story unfolds, Esther lives in the palace and has many people to assist her. Did she feel inner turmoil or pain? The tension of feeling, "I have what most women want, but what I had to go through to get it" may have been warring within.

Eventually there is a plot to kill all the Jewish people. Esther was Jewish but had never revealed that fact. Mordecai (another man determining her life choices) instructs Esther to present herself to the king and ask for favor and the salvation of her people. Esther becomes afraid and is told that just because she lives in the palace does not mean she will escape but that maybe the Lord had placed her in such a situation to save her people for such a time as this. Once again, Esther must die to self to save others.

Could that be you right now? Have you gone through something similar? To move forward in life, I encourage you to die to self to live free in Christ. Do you need to lay down the anger, feelings of dirtiness, and being used in order to grasp hold of beauty? Do you need to release your mourning of what "could have been" and allow Jesus to give you joy? Do you need to challenge your depression with shouts of praise?

Jewish people today still celebrate Purim, the name of the holiday to mark the time Esther won the right for them to fight back against those who wanted to extinguish them. Yes, Esther's choice to make the exchange still provides celebration for others. Could what you have gone through bring hope, comfort, and healing to others? Your exchange *will* impact many.

THE EXCHANGE

So how did David, Ruth, Joseph, and Esther all make the exchange? David cried out to the Lord and kept his heart pure. Ruth reached out to others during her pain and became faithful to love and help them. Joseph kept his eyes on God and hid the call in his heart to prevent others from stealing it. Esther died to self and trusted that God would vindicate her. Each one had an aspect in common. They refused to give up.

Galatians 6:9 states, "Let us not become weary in doing good, for at the proper time we will reap a harvest if we do not give up." Keep pushing forward. You are almost there! You have a reward and blessings in abundance waiting if you just keep going.

What is the most beautiful aspect that comes out of being broken? It is a statement Paul makes in Galatians 2:20: "I have been crucified with Christ and I no longer live, but Christ lives in me. The life I now live in the body, I live by faith in the son of God, who loved me and gave himself for me." May this become our anthem. Reread that verse out loud. Own it. Keep repeating it until you believe it—not simply with head knowledge but with heart knowledge. There is a difference between knowing something intellectually and believing in your spirit.

Are you becoming more beautiful? Have you exchanged your ashes for beauty? That process may necessitate crying out to God daily for a while until you feel the transformational moment. For others, the transformation may come without any pivotal moment but just through a slow conversion. I can already see the gray of your life turning into the beautiful ray of colored gemstones.

So, what can we expect after the exchange? Psalm 126:5–6 states, "Those who sow with tears will reap with songs of joy. Those who go out weeping, carrying seed to sow, will return with songs of joy, carrying sheaves with them." God will ask you to plant seed with the joy you have received.

CHAPTER 12

REFRESHING TIMES

Mountain top experiences are only possible
because we walked in the valley below and climbed up.

Mountain top experiences are powerful and breathtaking. They inspire us when we struggle in the valley. Witnessing God's mighty, miraculous, holistic healing and superior signs catapults us into a state of awe and excitement. Yet, we have learned that one cannot reside on the top all the time; that is not reality. Even Moses had to come back down.

High elevations are only possible if we have climbed up. Trekking to the top requires stamina, the ability to breathe differently, determination, and precise training. You have learned all of these qualities so far in this book, or at least I hope you have. I pray the Spirit has spoken to you, nudged you, and challenged you through this book and brought you to a place of peace. Your circumstances may not have changed, but you have. You now wait on divine intervention. You feel stronger than you ever thought you could be. However, you realize that this feeling arrived not by your doing, but by the grace of God. You are an overcomer!

As time draws on, and you continue to move forward, remember where you came from. God heals the pain but leaves the scars. Why are scars vital? They remind us of the story. It feels wonderful to share how you fell off your bike or were tackled in the neighborhood game of football and no longer experience the pain. Everyone can have a good laugh as they mentally visualize you flying through the air. Emotional scars are even more relevant. They remind us of the Lord's goodness, provision, healing, grace, favor, love, and presence. They are permanently seared in our minds, which increases trust. We remember how faithful God was, especially when we needed Him the most.

Your appreciation for God has grown to a depth never imagined. There's a rawness with your relationship with Him that you've never experienced before. I know. I've been there too. We can trust Him, count on Him, lean on Him, and cry out to Him.

Everything has a beginning and an ending. The only unchangeable is God Himself.

Ecclesiastes 3:1–8 reminds us,

> *There is a time for everything, and a season for every activity under the heavens: a time to be born and a time to die, a time to plant and a timed uproot, a time to kill and a time to heal, a time to tear down and a time to build, a time to weep and a time to laugh, a time to mourn and a time to dance, a time to scatter stones and a time to gather them, a time to embrace and a time to refrain from embracing, a time to search and a time to give up, a time to keep and a time to throw away, a time to tear and a time to mend, a time to be silent and a time to speak, a time to love and a time to hate, a time for war and a time for peace.*

As this passage demonstrates, there is a time for everything. Were you able to discern your life in the above? Your situation began, but it's also ending. I am so thankful that we have a God who understands, aren't you? No pit is too deep, and His arm is not too short.

I had a dream that included my husband, Kraig, and my dog, Kooper. A wolf was circling Kooper and then attacked him around the neck. I was crying and yelling for my husband to stop the attack since he was standing beside Kooper. My husband looked at me and instructed me to go higher. I turned around, and there was a stack of rocks. I began climbing, and I could hear the Spirit whisper in my ear, "Go higher. Higher." The Spirit kept urging me to climb higher. The wolf quit attacking Kooper and began to shift his attention to me. He walked around the other side of the rocks and taunted me with a question in a human voice. "You think I can't come up there, don't you?" The interesting aspect is, I knew he couldn't. The wolf was not fooling me. Fear that was prevalent earlier was quickly doused.

The Lord often speaks to us as we sleep. God uses dreams so that we cannot complicate the message. While awake, our mind tends to rationalize or justify what is revealed in order to comprehend it. In other words, we 'dumb down' what is revealed to be able to wrap our minds around it.

In this dream, my husband represented Jesus; my dog, Kooper, was the church plant, and the wolf was the devil. The devil was attacking the church plant, and the Lord was encouraging me to run to Him to prevent the enemy from taking me down also. I had to go higher in my relationship with Him for protection and security. When the church plant closed, it was devastating. This dream continually reminds me that no matter what the devil tries to do, as long as we stand on the Rock, then nothing—I repeat nothing—can overcome us. The Spirit was directing me towards Him, just as David cried to the Lord and said, "Lead me to the Rock that is higher than I" (Psalm 61:1–2). Furthermore, there was a time for God to build, then a time for me to walk away. When we recognize the time accurately, we are freed from the expectations we place on ourselves.

I pray that you have climbed the Rock and have gone higher throughout your journey. The view up there is much better than down below. Hopefully, you can see more spiritual things than mere earthly things. Don't lose sight of this view, but rather, keep your eyes fixed.

Romans 8:18 says, "I consider that our present sufferings are not worth comparing with the glory that will be revealed in us." Paul continues in verses 28–31,

> *And we know that in all things God works for the good of those that love him, who have been called according to his purpose. For those God foreknew he also predestined to become conformed to the image of his son, that he might be the firstborn among many brothers and sisters. And those he predestined, he also called; those he called, he also justified; those he justified, he also glorified. What, then, shall we say in response to these things? If God is for us, who can be against us?"*

God is for you. He has always been for you. He's never been mad at you. God can, will, and does turn everything to our good. Just as God turned my trial into a book, He will turn your situation into a blessing. Somehow. Someway. Someday.

A time of refreshing will come or has already begun for you. As Acts 3:19 states, "Repent, then, and turn to God, that your sins may be wiped out, that times are refreshing may come from the Lord." You have made it through the fire and are recovering from the effects of the heat. Fresh wind is blowing in your direction, providing for full breathing and the ability to move forward. All of this air is from God so you can run, play, laugh, and enjoy life again.

God will give you new life, new strength, and possibly even a new direction. I received a new understanding through my journey, from Paul's words in Philippians 4:12–13: "I know what it is to be in need, and I know what it is to have plenty. I have learned the secret of being content in any and every situation, whether well fed or hungry, whether living in plenty or in want. I can do all this through him who gives me strength." We can rest assured that contentment comes from the Lord alone. Refreshing times do not originate merely from human strength, but from divine intervention and provision.

STATE OF TRANSITION

A transition period exists where one learns how to live again and fully enjoy life. It feels strange at first when the refreshing times begin. A sense of trepidation may occur. You may feel some type of anxiety or fear, waiting for something else bad to happen. When and if these thoughts and feelings arise, quickly let go of them. Do not allow them to gain a foothold. This type of thought process transpires if your past has been chaotic and unsettled. Continue to remind yourself that your current state is not the same as your past.

Furthermore, you may grapple with how to act or what to do with yourself. My advice? Live! Enjoy the refreshing times. Jesus came that we might have life and in abundance (John 10:10). Take time to enjoy the little things. Spend time with family and friends. Engage in life-giving activities. Your ventures will not resemble mine. What brings you joy? Do those things. Enjoy life.

Bask in the blessings God has provided. Stop to smell the roses.

Continue to read your Bible, pray, go to church, and spend quality quiet time with God. Do not lose sight of who God has been and continues to be for you. This is not the time to pull back. While you may not feel as desperate as you previously did, do not lose sight of His perspective and His place of prominence in your life. You have a new appreciation for God, and your smile reflects His love. God wants to bless you. Receive it! You feel good, and your faith is renewed and strengthened. You are full of new possibilities, and your horizon looks promising. God will fill you full of Him.

It remains imperative that you appreciate the refreshing times. They will not last forever. Remember, everything ends. When the Israelites made it to the Promised Land, they celebrated and praised the Lord. They enjoyed the new life. However, the hard work came next. They had to conquer the Promised Land.

The journey you just went through or are still endeavoring to walk out victoriously will not be the only time in your life when trials enter the picture. Jesus informs us that we will have tribulations, but we must not fear them because He has already taken care of them (John 16:33). Remember, you were truly never alone. This will give you confidence the next time you face a hardship. Hopefully, it will prevent a future trial from feeling as difficult to endure. The more you trust, lean on, and learn to cry out to the Lord, the less likely you are to relive the process of being broken and rebuilt.

REACH OUT TO OTHERS

We are not filled with new life only for ourselves. We experience renewal, refreshing, and revival so the Lord can use us to reach out to others. Our purpose is to know Him (which this journey has assisted in, I hope) and to make known His resurrection power to others (Philippians 3:10). If my time of pain brings freedom to one person, then it was all worth it. If the journey to wholeness and healing for me resulted in your transformation, then what the enemy meant to use to destroy me has brought life to you. That is the goal of this journey called life.

The ability to relate to others is foundational to our faith walk. As 2 Corinthians 1:3–4 states, "Praise be to the God and father of our Lord Jesus Christ, the father of compassion and the God of all comfort, who comforts us in all our troubles, so that we can comfort those in any trouble with the comfort we ourselves received from God." This is a time when God prompts you to help others. The wisdom you gained—you must share. Your mess has become your ministry. Your trial has become your testimony. This is how many people enter ministry.

During times of refreshing, people are so filled with God that rivers of living water flow from them. There's no dam to stop the flow of God, so people in close proximity receive the benefit. Have you ever wondered why people are led toward each other spiritually? Well, people are drawn because deep calls out to deep. In other words, someone sees in you what they are currently experiencing. You need to impart the wisdom you have gained through your trial in order to encourage them.

Right now, there is a sense that the Spirit is enlightening you to reach out to a person. A name might have just popped into your thoughts. You may not have known that he or she has been going through a difficult season, but discernment has revealed this. Do not feel afraid about what to say. Just obey. Let the person know what you experienced, and then speak the word of encouragement. Perfection is overrated. When you were struggling, would it have mattered if the person spoke complete sentences and used the exact words? No. You would have just felt thrilled that the Lord saw you and ministered to you. Remember where you came from, and share from your heart.

The first time the Lord transformed me resulted in the birth of a ministry. You may feel led to do some ministry at this moment—begin an outreach at your church or out of your home. This can be exciting and a little scary. Can I offer a few words of advice from experience? Great! First, pray through what you think the Spirit is speaking. What is meant by pray through? Write down what you sense thus far. Then, every day during your prayer time, ask the Lord to bring further clarity and to fill in the needed details. Ask your pastor or trusted friend to pray with you regarding this endeavor.

Next, ask the Lord to reveal to you when to step out. Waiting on God's timing was not my strong quality. Truth be told, it still isn't. However, moving ahead of the Lord can be just as devastating as not stepping out at all. Ask Him for confirmation. When you receive it, then wait until the door opens. If you are married, make sure your spouse agrees—another hard lesson I learned along this journey.

One last piece of wisdom: keep your eyes on Jesus. He will provide everything you need to perform His will. Never forget that it is His strength and idea in you, not yours. The results are up to Him. Simply remain obedient and give Him glory.

What happens when you feel led to speak or write your message publicly? First, write it down. I have observed many wonderful people who have powerful testimonies but have not whittled their story down to a manageable presentation, so unfortunately, they lost people's attention. When the message is too cumbersome, people shut down. Their ability and desire to listen disappears. This can negatively impact your willingness to share again if you observe their distractions. Write and rewrite your story until it flows. Have a thirty second 'elevator pitch'—something the length that one could tell a stranger in an elevator ride—which summarizes it. People can ask follow-up questions for you to elaborate on, but you cannot reconnect people once they disengage.

When you have come to a place of peace with your journey and feel confident you have honed it, then ask the Lord to open doors for you to deliver it. When I say honed, again, I am not referring to perfection, but the ability to identify key elements. One way to begin this process is to communicate the message to your pastor and ask if you can share during a prayer meeting or Bible study. Another idea is to record yourself speaking and put it on social media. Technology has provided the means for many open doors. Just make sure you are ready for it through the Spirit's leading. You can even inform friends and let them know you are willing to encourage others if they know anyone experiencing something similar. Also, convey to them your availability to speak at events they host.

CAUTION DURING TIMES OF REFRESHMENT

Do not become so worked up emotionally that you forget wisdom. When the Lord called me into ministry, it ended up unfolding differently than what I had envisioned. I could have avoided frustration, impatience, and discouragement had wisdom been utilized. I thought every evangelist did the same thing, the same way, as the only ones known to me were television evangelists. Through trial and error, lessons were learned.

The world draws us to want fame and for our name to be recognized. Even with good and godly intentions, pride can enter. Our journey then becomes more about building our ministry than about building the Kingdom. Put your dream on the altar. Die to what you sense God is wanting you to do and then keep it there. What is meant by that? You must remain content and continue to serve the Lord even if your dream never comes to pass. Frustration and discouragement enter when we become so focused on trying to open doors for our dream to materialize instead of keeping Jesus as our first love.

One protective measure to remain on track is to obtain a mentor. Allow him or her to speak wisdom, understanding, and guidance into your journey. This can prevent pitfalls and future heartache. Plus, the Lord identified this biblical pattern for us with relationships such as Paul with Timothy and Elizabeth with Mary.

Enjoy the refreshing moments. Embrace them, bask in them, and be thankful for them. What happens when you feel as though you took a step backward? Does this mean the time has passed? No, it just means you must refocus and continue to grow.

CHAPTER 13

RESIDUAL EFFECTS

"Don't give up. Normally it is the
last key on the ring which opens the door."
—Fritz Cherry

Life can be quite a journey with all the twists, turns, upside downs, and straightaways. Just when we think a situation is resolved, a project mastered, or a weakness overcome, we are bombarded with emotions and thoughts that appear to come from nowhere. These past sensations stop us in our tracks and leave us feeling confused. "Wait, didn't I already deal with this? Why has this returned?" This is normal. Take a deep breath and let us examine why you are experiencing residual effects.

REASONS FOR RESIDUAL EFFECTS

Multiple reasons exist why residual effects enter the equation on our journey of transformation. As I detail these, ask the

Spirit to reveal the reason in your life. Once you have a better understanding and clearer picture of what precipitated them, then implement the suggestions on how to address these problems.

First, we have an enemy who is our accuser (Revelation 12:10). Satan buffets us to cave in to him and continues to bring up our past to enslave us again. I remember after the Lord delivered me from shame, the enemy would taunt me with, "You think you have been freed, but what about..." and he would remind me of a sin or weakness. The more I ignored him, the less he utilized this method. Friends, do not give in to this! The enemy knows he is a defeated foe, and that is why he fights so hard. Recognize his tactics, and do not fall prey to them.

Another reason for residual effects may be that old habits die hard. When we respond a certain way for days, months, or even years, reactions settle in as a way of life. They become subconsciously ingrained and must be uprooted. These customs can even impact our personalities. John Ortberg in his book *Soul Keeping* believes that "The deeper freedom—the freedom that the soul needs—is the freedom for becoming the person I was designed to be."[13] When you challenge and replace these habits, then you develop into who you truly are. This may be the reason you even perceived changes within while reading this book. Awareness is half the battle. When you notice repeated patterns, make a conscious choice to change. Replace the detrimental response with a godly reply.

When someone returns from one's past, or a similar situation occurs, then residual effects may surface. These flashbacks, as they are called, can feel intense and overwhelming. They have the potential to last for days or even trigger us to return to bondage.

Old feelings and thought patterns push through new revelation and overpower it. The closer in proximity to the event, the more difficult it is to reframe what is transpiring. However, all is not lost. Reach out to a trusted friend and process what is unfolding. Do not attempt to 'figure it out' on your own. Thankfully, the more time that lapses, the decreased ability flashbacks have in taking hold in the moment. One more piece of wisdom, some of you may be 'delayed responders.' What is this? When something occurs, it does not sink in until a day or two, even a week later. Then you begin to experience the above and become confused because there appears no reason for it. The same response needs to coincide with the counsel offered above. Process what transpired, and then continue to wage war.

Misery loves company. Others may attempt to drag you back into your past, which only keeps it fresh in your mind. If you were the instigator of pain, then knowing who you are in Christ is imperative. Jesus has forgiven you and has removed your sins. If someone else harmed you, and others are wanting to vindicate you or keep you stirred up, distance yourself from this person or people and connect with others who speak life to you. Forgiving others frees you from falling into this snare. Avoid situations where gossip erupts, and do not comment on the event or person. Again, this only heightens your memory and the pain associated with it.

If residual effects continue to surface, shame may be the underlying cause. Shame can creep in when we least expect it to and can wreak havoc. I had been assistant presbyter for only about a year when a situation occurred during credential interviews. One of the other ministers in the room made a joke that slighted women in ministry. (I do not think he realized what he said was offensive.) I immediately pulled back from the table and felt so insecure. Throughout the day I struggled feeling unworthy of being in ministry. During my evening walk, I asked the Lord to reveal what was going on, since I thought this type of issue was resolved. The Spirit whispered to my heart, "You are experiencing shame. You feel like you are not good enough and do not measure up." In that one moment, past issues surfaced through circumstances tied with shame. Do certain comments from others cause you to run and hide? That is shame. Look at Adam and Eve. How did they respond to shame? They hid. Ask the Lord to remove the chains of this evil expression.

Similar to shame is guilt. Sometimes guilt surfaces when things are going well. We wonder if we deserve good things and what other people will think of our blessings, especially if our behavior caused part of our brokenness. Someone reading this is feeling guilty for being in a time of refreshment while the person you hurt is still experiencing the pain. I want to remind you that God restored you. *Restored* is past tense. Embrace your new location. Take off the grave clothes of guilt like Lazarus's were removed when he came out of the tomb. The time for correction is over, and it is time for a new life.

Another reason for residual effects is the need for a deeper level of healing. Our lives are like onions—we have multiple layers. To arrive at the core, one must peel away a layer at a time—so, too, with holistic healing. Sometimes the pain is at a depth that requires some progress and an increased faith to allow the light of Christ to shine into it. It is easier to trust the Lord when He has already proven Himself faithful in a lesser situation. Plus, we become more comfortable inviting Him into our darkest secrets when we know His love and that His motive is for complete wholeness. If this is your experience, prepare for another level of freedom.

One last reason residual effects surface is that when we step out into something new, the enemy attacks us with trying to bring us back to the past. This happens time after time. If the enemy cannot stop our obedience, then he attacks our mental and emotional stability. The forces of the enemy of our soul may drop thoughts into your mind to see which ones you latch onto, such as, "You think you can do that after what you have done? Who do you think you are? What if you fail? Did the Lord really say to do that? If God did not rescue you in the harmful situation, why do you think He is going to come through if you step out now?" These are just a few of the numerous statements personally heard in my own head throughout my life or have been reported to me in counseling sessions. If we do not fall prey to them, then he continues to "up the ante" until he finds one that sticks. This is a good time to remind you that *you* choose your thoughts. You cannot stop thoughts from coming in, but you *can* decide which ones on which to meditate. View thoughts like ocean waves— they come and go; do not ride them.

It is important, but not essential, to know the *why* of residual effects. If you cannot relate to any of the above reasons, then pray and ask the Spirit to bring revelation. If you still do not have understanding, then move on. Do not become entangled with the *why*. Remember, you have an enemy who desires nothing more than for you to be bound, and he just may be using this question to produce a stronghold.

HOW TO HANDLE RESIDUAL EFFECTS

How can we respond to the pain that rears its ugly head? Quickly relinquish it to the Lord. Do not partner with it! Cry out like David, and do not fight in your own strength. What method did the prophet Jahaziel give King Jehoshaphat and the Israelites? Let me remind you. In 2 Chronicles 20:17 he says, "You will not have to fight this battle. Take up your positions; stand firm and see the deliverance the Lord will give you, Judah and Jerusalem. Do not be afraid; do not be discouraged. Go out to face them tomorrow, and the Lord will be with you."

First, they were reminded that *the battle was not theirs*. At times, we think we must change. However, you and I are unable to thoroughly alter ourselves. Only the power of the Spirit can refresh our emotions and reconstruct our thinking. Only in surrender do we gain the victory.

Next, the prophet instructs Israel to *take up their positions*. They were to strategically locate themselves to have the advantage. Usually, this meant to be at a higher elevation in order gain visibility of the encroaching army. What does this mean for us? We are to move to a position of humility. From this view, we can see with spiritual eyes and the mind of Christ. First Peter 4:6 urges us, "Humble yourselves, therefore, under God's mighty hand, that he may lift you up in due time." What does this look like? Instead of trying to figure things out, we fall to our knees. We say, "Have your way, O God." From this place marching orders are given.

What is the prophet's third command to Israel? *Stand firm!* We have already identified multiple ways to stand firm on the battle ground. Let me name a few. Be still and know that He is

God (Psalm 46:10). Invite Him into your space to reveal to you who He is and to remind you what He has already accomplished in your life. Read Scripture, praise the Lord, and worship Him. Remember, worship wins the war. Ask others to pray for you and with you. At this point, include fasting into your life if you have not already. I love what Staci Wallace stresses in her book, *Fueled by Fire*: "Do not retreat, but reload!"[14] Keep standing. Remember, sometimes after a fire is stifled, small embers remain. It is imperative that firefighters stay around to douse the embers if they flame up again. Pull out the "water" of the Spirit and aim away until the only aspect that remains is a charred remnant of the enemy.

Fourth, the prophet instructs Israel to *see the deliverance of the Lord*. One way to observe His goodness and faithfulness is to go back and read previous journal entries written during times of healing. Remind yourself what God has previously spoken to you. Reread specific chapters in this book for repetitive benefit.

The fifth instruction is, *Do not be afraid!* The Israelites were afraid to die or lose their land. This is such an issue for us isn't it? Why is fear so prevalent? Honestly, because we do not want to experience pain or lose anything of value. I know we all suffer with this. In the Western world, we balk at almost anything that will trigger us to become uncomfortable. This results in the need to control. I have found that the main way to address this is to die to self and my expectations. When the apostles were arrested and threatened with further harm if they continued to speak about Jesus, how did they respond? With fear? Not at all. They prayed for more of the Spirit to speak boldly (Acts 4). May we respond in similar fashion: "Lord, give us the boldness to overcome ALL forces of evil that come against us."

Obviously, the king and Israelites needed further encouragement to not give up. The prophet told them, *Do not be discouraged.* The same cheer is offered here. Do not give up! You have made it this far. Have you ever watched a football game while it is snowing—I mean, *really* snowing where you can barely see the end zone? What if, on the fourth down instead of pushing it, they settled for a field goal? What if they figured some progress thus far was good enough? Even though it is not complete freedom, it is better than where we were. What if the end of your insecurities, anger, confusion, or any other negative expression was just a half yard away? You cannot see it because of the snow, but you are almost at the end zone. Would you make one last ditch effort? Sure! Break that invisible plane where the touchdown occurs. You can do it! Fight the good fight of faith!

Then the prophet exclaimed, "Go out and *face* them!" The Israelites had to face the vast army to defeat them. You too must face the forces of the enemy to overcome them. The only way to freedom is to face what hinders you. Running from it (whatever "it" is for you—shame, guilt, flashbacks, deeper pain, or new spiritual level) will prolong this journey. When you push down the emotions or ignore the red flags, they will surface in other ways with the potential to trigger additional pain, only to have to repeat this process of healing.

The last section of the verse, *The Lord will be with you,* was the reminder that they were not alone. "If God be for you, who can be against you?" (Romans 8:31). Dear friend, you are not and have never been alone. A multitude of Scriptures inform us of this very thing. Battle by reading every one of them. Pull out your Bible concordance and read how the Lord is always with you. Post sticky notes all around your home. Place these Scriptures on your phone, computer, or tablet. Speak "I am not alone" over and over your life, until it takes root in your spirit.

Walking out freedom may have setbacks, but as Staci Wallace in a podcast interview with me declared, "When you have a setback, do not take a step back. Because it might just be a setup for your come back."[15]

CHAPTER 14

TRANSFORMATIONAL LIVING

"God is looking for those with whom
He can do the impossible—what a pity that we plan
only the things that we can do by ourselves."
—A. W. Tozer

We have come to the end of this journey together, with its beauty and humility resulting in a display of God's glory. The course does not end here, though. Much remains to be written on your heart and in your life. Paul reminds us in 2 Corinthians 3:18, "And we all, who with unveiled faces contemplate with the Lord's glory, are being transformed into his image with ever-increasing glory, which comes from the Lord, who is the Spirit."

God does not cease the development of His children when healing from the past is complete or when freedom from strongholds transpires. No, brothers and sisters, He longs for more! *El Shaddai*—God Almighty, God the All-Sufficient One, desires to increase the depth of our knowledge of Him, to bestow upon us more of His power and authority and to release us with His glory as our leader. The great I AM treasures every moment that we embrace His presence and is pleased when we slide our hand into His, as we jointly face each day.

Even as I type this, I sense the nearness of our Lord. There is a sweet Spirit that engulfs our intellects and infuses joy into our emotions. We are more than just human, but superhuman when we accept Jesus to be our Savior. Many times, people accept Jesus into their lives, but they stop there. Salvation is attained, and life unfolds. Yet God does not want to just be a prayer you recited to have your name written in the Lamb's Book of Life. Again, salvation is a miracle—one to thank Him for daily. Jesus wants you to invite Him to be Lord of your life. This is when He has your permission to take you from glory to glory. Someone reading that last comment just gasped. You think, "He does not need my permission," but He longs for it. Let me unpack this statement.

When we accept Christ into our heart, He becomes our Savior. He alone forgives all sin and restores our relationship with the Father. Jesus bought us with the price of His life. This is redemption. Oh, what a majestic redemption! There is nothing more precious than the blood of Jesus. We gain entrance into eternity through our faith in Him. Can you picture the streets paved with gold and the vast array of beautiful gemstones on the gates? I love to visualize what heaven looks like.

As the next step in our walk with Jesus, we must elevate Him as Lord. Many Scriptures instruct us to love the Lord with all our heart, soul, mind, and strength (Deuteronomy 6:5; 10:12; Matthew 22:37; Mark 12:30; Luke 10:27). To accomplish this, He *must* become and remain our first love. This entails dying daily to any wants, needs, and desires of ours that would keep us from grabbing hold of His will and plans for us.

The only way we will go from glory to glory is if we remain in Him. We cannot expect His blessings without keeping Him first on our journey. Have you have ever driven for a family vacation and the car was packed with no more room for a single item? For one more bag to fit, you would have to leave something else behind. This is what happens with our spiritual commitments over time. We start with the Lord in our vehicle. There is excitement about the destination. Our energy is high, emotions are positive, and our faith unhindered. Yet as our schedules fill up, life unfolds, and days turn into months we replace Him with carpools, a glass of wine, sleeping in, or technological gadgets.

Why do we tolerate such a shift of focus when we began with great intentions? A litany of reasons exists to answer that question, and they differ based on seasons of life. If you are a college student, then studying for finals or social gatherings can replace time spent with the Lord. If you are a single parent, the burdens of life in general trigger exhaustion, and finding time to spiritually feed oneself is pushed to the back burner. If you work as a businessperson, then late-night meetings or travel out of town precipitate missing church services and Bible study. If you serve as a minister, the needs of others replace time spent sitting at the feet of Jesus. We exchange time in His presence with doing what He calls us to do. What has it been in your life? What strategy has the enemy used to remove the Lord as your first love? For me, it has been unmet expectations, running a business and ministry, cares of the world, and listening to the wrong voices, even well-meaning ones.

Jesus reminded the church at Ephesus that they were missing the point:

> *I know your deeds, your hard work and your perseverance. I know that you cannot tolerate wicked people, that you have tested those who claim to be apostles but are not, and have found them false. You have persevered and have endured hardships for my name, and have not grown weary. Yet I hold this against you; You have forsaken the love you had at first.*   —Revelation 2:2–4

Here, Jesus is informing the Ephesians that they have been working hard in His name. He sees they are doing spiritual activities and continue to do so. He acknowledges and commends these actions but then declares they have decreased in their love for Him. Why is this vital? Because if they did not repent and return to previous ways, then slowly they too would become 'religious' and not in relationship focused on Him—going through the motions with no connection to the life-giving source. Eventually, they would die out. He declares in verse 5, "Consider how far you have fallen! Repent and do the things you did at first. If you do not repent, I will come to you and remove your lampstand from its place." Jesus is serious about being and remaining our first love. He is the source of all life. He is not just one resource that we can turn to, but our *only* one!

This is how we live transformational. If we want to continue to go deeper with the Lord, we must come up higher in our spiritual walk and be used mightily for Kingdom purposes—and keep Jesus as our first love.

How do we abide by this mindset and commitment? Every morning make a conscious choice to choose to love Him. You can even say out loud, "Jesus, I embrace Your plan for today. Help me die to any of my own wants that would keep me from walking in obedience to Your leadership. Help me to shine Your light and express Your character with the fruit of the Spirit." As Jesus reveals in John 14:21–23,

> *Whoever has my commands and keeps them is the one who loves me. The one who loves me will be loved by my Father, and I will love them and show myself to them. Then Judas (not Judas Iscariot) said, 'But Lord, why do you intend to show yourself to us and not to the world?' Jesus replied, 'Anyone who loves me will obey my teaching. My Father will love them, and we will come to them and make our home with them."*

What are those commands? To love the Lord with our whole being. But it goes one step further. To be true disciples of Christ, we must deny ourselves, pick up our cross and follow Him (Matthew 16:24). This book has already laid out multiple examples, like forgiving others who hurt us, finding peace with God, exchanging our ashes for beauty, and pleasing God instead of people. These continued practices allow us to witness the glory of the Lord. You have experienced this when, instead of staying home to watch football, you attended the prayer meeting, and the Spirit ministered to you. You left with gratitude that you followed through with your commitment instead of feeding your flesh, which wanted to remain seated on the couch with a warm fire. Or another example, you went to the hospital to sit with a friend instead of tackling your to-do list for the day.

Further, we must remain attached to the Vine, as Jesus's analogy in John 15 describes. In verse 2 Jesus speaks of God's actions: "He cuts off every branch in me that bears no fruit, while every branch that does bear fruit he prunes so that it will be even more fruitful." Let's be honest. This verse does not lend toward good feelings. "Cut off" and "prune" do not make us want to run to Him. However, we all pursue Him for the fruit. We long for freedom, for peace, to be utilized as a vessel, and to witness miracles, signs, and wonders. To accomplish this, we must allow the Lord to remove areas in our lives that do not bring life. Perhaps those "areas" may include a friendship, a job, a relationship, or a ministry. They are dead, but you hang onto them for comfort or familiarity. We have things in our lives that need pruning. Attitudes like, "What can you do for me?" must be removed. Behaviors out of selfish ambition need to detach. Fears of the future must be dislodged. Pruning can be painful, yet it is worth the fruit that is produced to be taken from glory to glory.

The last area to help us remain connected to the Lord as our first love and to live transformational is to implement spiritual disciplines into our daily lives. Spiritual disciplines, in and of themselves, do not take us deeper with the Lord. Remember the church at Ephesus? I love how Adele Ahlberg Calhoun puts it in her book *Spiritual Disciplines Handbook: Practices that Transform Us*: "Spiritual practices don't give us 'spiritual brownie points' or help us 'work the system' for a passing grade from God. They simply put us in a place where we can begin to notice God and respond to his word in us."[16] Spiritual disciplines do not warrant a reward from God. We merely use them to invite Him into our lives. Many times, people have placed expectations in their 'name it and claim it' method and have come away broken with unmet needs. I hear it frequently: "But I prayed and spent time with the Lord! He owes me!"

There was a time I was obedient to the Lord and stepped way out of my comfort zone, which cost me financially. I was so discouraged. My mentor at the time asked me a poignant question, "Do you feel that God let you down?" I responded honestly with "Yes." By the look on his face, I knew that was the incorrect answer. Immediately, he responded with "God does not owe you anything." The weight of that truth hit me like a two-ton piece of steel in my heart. I repented right there.

Just because we do something for God does not mean He is required to respond the way we want Him to or the way we think He should. Did that step of obedience bring fruit? Absolutely. Lives were changed and impacted because of my obedience. A lady who attended the services was possibly healed of cancer. (I say possibly because I did not obtain medical proof, but she is on my prayer team, so that is good enough for me.) Did the Lord provide financially the way I thought He should to meet my expenses? No, but within a week, all accounts were paid, and a tremendous lesson on humility transpired. Our obedience opens the door for Him to enter.

Here is a list of spiritual disciplines to assist in living a transformational life.

- Attend a Bible Study
- Obtain an accountability partner
- Pray
- Repent
- Have daily devotions
- Conduct an in-depth study of Scripture
- Disciple someone else

- Fast
- Take Communion
- Meditate
- Memorize Scripture
- Rest
- Take retreats
- Honor a time of Sabbath
- Serve others
- Tithe
- Praise and show thankfulness
- Worship

As you can see, this list incorporates activities done in community like attending a Bible study, obtaining an accountability partner, discipling someone, and serving others. The New Testament Church (throughout Acts) is a great study on how walking in unity and spending quality time with other like-minded people produces spiritual fruit.

Other activities on the list center around personal responsibility (although some can also be done with others, I am referring more to a heart issue), like tithing, praise, worship, taking a Sabbath, resting when needed, fasting, praying, and repentance. If we look to Jesus as our example, there were multiple times He withdrew to pray to God or to just rest (Luke 5:16). During such times, personal renewal transpires when God provides personal ministry to us such as new life, direction, and correction.

To know Christ more, we must know the Word. There is no shortcut in this area. Time spent daily in His Word will increase our understanding and knowledge. Meditation and Scripture memorization aids helps get the Word inside us and gives us the potential to walk out His ways.

Purchase a book or do further research on spiritual disciplines. The more you invest in this area, the more your spiritual formation will benefit. Information for the book by Adele referenced is in the endnotes.

The subject of perfectionism is imperative to mention at this juncture. Yes, the Lord desires to reveal Himself to us. He wants to move us from glory to glory. He yearns for His children to invite Him into every area of life. He awaits our surrender to promote us. But most of all, He just wants a real relationship with us. He appeals to each one of us to come as we are. He entreats us to sit with Him and yield to His plan, His ways, and His love. We are not called to be perfect or have everything figured out before we can approach His throne. Far from it! We can live from glory to glory when we allow the Giver of Life, the Price of Peace, *Adonai* access to the depths of our souls and allow the Light of the World to shine through us. If we can grasp the truth that "Greater is He that is in us than he that is in the world," (1 John 4:4), then we become unstoppable!

God has graced us with power and authority in the spiritual realm to bring the kingdom of heaven to earth (Matthew 6:10). No weapon formed against us can prosper as we enter the enemy's camp and take back what he has stolen (Isaiah 54:17). Friends, our loved ones are counting on us. The cities we live in desperately await believers who will stand up and fight. Nations are moaning at the weight of darkness. We do not have time to remain in bondage to our past. The future awaits our obedience now. Decisions we make today will project what lies ahead for us and those around us.

We can live from glory to glory as He transforms us daily into His image. Doing so is all about Him; it always has been and will always be. His transformation in us has never been about merely what we do, but what He desires to do for us and through us. Rise and take your place on the battleground as we stand linked arm and arm. Are you ready? Let us do this!

ENDNOTES

1   Simon Tugwell, *The Beatitudes: Soundings in Christian Tradition* (Springfield, IL: Templegate Publishers, 1980), 130.

2   Peter Scazzero, *Emotionally Healthy Spirituality: Unleash a Revolution in Your Life in Christ* (Nashville: Thomas Nelson, 2006), 56.

3   Michael W. Smith, "Waymaker," Lyrics.com, accessed December 2, 2020, https://www.lyrics.com/track/36189713/Michael+W.+Smith/Waymaker.

4   Casting Crowns, "East to West," YouTube Official Lyric Video, accessed December 8, 2020, https://youtu.be/TnkkZLdjf9Y.

5   "Heir," Merriam-Webster, accessed January 7, 2021, https://www.merriam-webster.com/dictionary/heir.

6   Ibid.

7   Ibid.

8   Merrill C. Tenney, *The Gospel of John*, vol. 9 of *The Expositor's Bible Commentary*, ed. Frank E. Gaebelein (Grand Rapids, MI: Zondervan, 1981), 28.

9   Ibid.

10 Leon Morris, *Hebrews*, vol. 12 of *The Expositor's Bible Commentary*, ed. Frank E. Gaebelein (Grand Rapids, MI: Zondervan, 1981), 44.

11 Brennan Manning with Jim Hancock, *Posers, Fakers, & Wannabes*, (Colorado Springs: NavPress, 2003), 112.

12 Merriam-Webster, "Self-Pity," accessed December 9, 2020, http://www.merriam-webster.com/self-pity.

13 John Ortberg, *Soul Keeping: Caring for the Most Important Part of You* (Grand Rapids, MI: Zondervan, 2014), 147.

14 Staci Wallace, *Fueled by Fire: Becoming a Woman of Courage, Faith and Influence* (Grand Rapids, MI: Chosen Books, 2020), 205.

15 "Living in the Light with Dr. Kristi Lemley," January 19, 2021, CPN Shows, accessed January 25, 2021, https://CPNshows.com/KristiLemley.

16 Adele Ahlberg Calhoun, *Spiritual Disciplines Handbook: Practices that Transform Us* (Downers Grove, IL: InterVarsity Press, 2005), 19.

BEAUTY FROM ASHES
Donna Sparks

In a transparent and powerful manner, the author reveals how the Lord took her from the ashes of a life devastated by failed relationships and destructive behavior to bring her into a beautiful and powerful relationship with Him. The author encourages others to allow the Lord to do the same for them.

Donna Sparks is an Assemblies of God evangelist who travels widely to speak at women's conferences and retreats. She lives in Tennessee.

www.story-of-grace.com

www.facebook.com/
  donnasparksministries/

www.facebook.com/
  AuthorDonnaSparks/

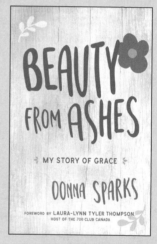

ISBN: 978-1-61036-252-8

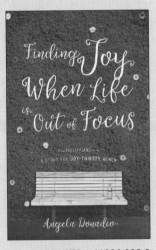

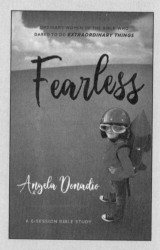